Randy Trabold poses with his cameras in 1966. The Rolleiflex is ready for action while his beloved Speed Graphic rests on the desk before him.

IMAGES
of America

RANDY TRABOLD'S
NORTHERN BERKSHIRE COUNTY

Edited by Dr. Tony Gengarelly
Massachusetts College of Liberal Arts Book Project

ARCADIA
PUBLISHING

Published by Arcadia Publishing
Charleston, South Carolina

Library of Congress Catalog Card Number: 2002117431

For all general information contact Arcadia Publishing at:
Telephone 843-853-2070
Fax 843-853-0044
E-mail sales@arcadiapublishing.com
For customer service and orders:
Toll-Free 1-888-313-2665

Visit us on the Internet at www.arcadiapublishing.com

Seen for miles around northern Berkshire County, the tower atop Mount Greylock sparkles in the winter sun.

CONTENTS

ACKNOWLEDGMENTS

The fine and performing arts majors from Massachusetts College of Liberal Arts (MCLA) who created the captions and chapter introductions for this volume, of course, deserve special recognition: Tim Bancroft, Jay Burnett, Jenn Dennis, Shea Kiley, Megan Laverty, Silvia Lazala, Jessica LeCours, Greg Mitchell, Rich Neyland, Christina Noell, Mark Olesak, Meghan O'Reilly, Adam Park, Lorna Rawlings, Cat Robinson, Motiryo Samuel, Elizabeth Thorpe, Jillian Tremblay, and Garvin White. Special thanks are due to the team of assistant editors: Megan Laverty, Jessica LeCours, Greg Mitchell, and Motiryo Samuel.

This book project also benefited from those students in years past who helped organize and display portions of the Randy Trabold Photograph Collection: Kim Alice, Erin Baynes, Cassie Dailey, Nancy Hughes, Michael Hutchinson, Robyn Mahoney, Jennifer Marden, and Jo-Anne La Vigne. Special appreciation is extended to Kim Alice, who edited and contributed significantly to the catalog for On the Scene: An Exhibition of Randy Trabold's Berkshire Photographs.

We are forever indebted to Ida Trabold for the use of the Randy Trabold photographs that form the basis of this book. This project was able to take advantage of the Randy Trabold Photograph Collection at MCLA, a bequest from Ida in 2001. We also benefited from access to more than 1,000 photographs in Ida's personal collection, including Randy Trabold memorabilia, that she so generously loaned. We also wish to thank Allen Morrill for making the resources of both the Freel Library and the Randy Trabold Photograph Collection available. Fond remembrance as well as thanks go to Ann Terryberry for her assistance in the early stages of exploring the Randy Trabold Photograph Collection. We also appreciate the assistance of Eugene Michalenko, who suggested the idea for an Arcadia publication and graciously shared his local history knowledge.

We are very grateful for the generous assistance of many people at MCLA and in the northern Berkshire County community, too numerous to mention here. The extraordinary efforts of Karen DeOrdio in the preparation of the book's master text, of Susan Denault in the organization of archival materials for the students, and of Maynard Seider, who graciously shared his local history library and expertise, must be especially noted. We also extend our thanks to Dennis Tash, Glenn Lawson, and Linda Kaufmann for their noteworthy contributions.

Finally, three sources upon which we relied and to which we are very indebted are Boxcar Media's Web site RandyTrabold.com and Joe Manning's two excellent volumes, Steeples and Disappearing into North Adams.

Grand marshall Randy Trabold rides with his wife, Ida, and two grandchildren in the 1971 Fall Foliage Festival parade.

INTRODUCTION

Randy Trabold needs no introduction to his many friends and admirers. Nearly 25 years after his untimely death in 1980, Randy is still remembered inside and outside northern Berkshire County. Many of the thousands of photographs taken during his 44-year career as a photojournalist continue to appear in the *North Adams Transcript* as well as other newspapers, books, and journals. This book is dedicated to his remarkable photographic accomplishments and to the history and memories he recorded for his own and future generations.

P. Randolph Trabold (known to nearly everyone as Randy) was born on September 4, 1917. During his formative years, Randy spent a great deal of time in the studio of his father, Peter Trabold, a photographer of note in the North Adams area. In 1935, at the age of 18, Randy became a news photographer at the *North Adams Transcript* and made all of northern Berkshire County his studio. Until he retired from the newspaper in 1979, he created a pictorial record of events that ranged from hard-breaking news to human-interest features; from fires, accidents, and natural disasters to local holidays and celebrations; and from images of people under duress to portraits of beauty queens and candid shots of children. Artistry and humanity—including a wonderful sense of humor—shine through all his pictures. Randy loved the local landscape and captured its many features with a patiently aesthetic eye. His seasonal shots, especially those of the long Berkshire winters, provided opportunity for some interesting and witty inventions. Many of his photographs received special recognition and awards from the major news organizations of his day, including the New England Associated Press and National Press Photographers Association. At a testimonial dinner for Randy in September 1979, U.S. Rep. Silvio Conte caught the spirit of Trabold's work with these words, later read into the Congressional Record: "What sets him apart is that he brings a measure of skill, creativity and sensitivity to his work that is anything but common. . . . He has a fine eye for taking an ordinary subject and making it into an extraordinary picture. He also has a rare sensitivity to people, and this sensitivity colors all of his work."

First and foremost Randy Trabold was a news photographer. Trabold's editor at the *Transcript*, Jim Hardman, once commented that Randy was "one of the best reporters, if not the best" he had had on his staff. Randy's wife of many years, Ida, concurs: "Randy was definitely a news photographer. We got calls at all hours with people telling him about a story. No one could be on the phone for too long at a time, because Randy didn't want to miss a story." At six feet three inches tall, he was a conspicuous part of nearly every important event throughout his north county beat. This commentary from Peter Gosselin, one of Trabold's colleagues at the *Transcript* who describes Randy covering a late-night automobile accident during a rainstorm, is especially worth recounting: "Emergency crews barely arrive before they are joined by a hulking man with a camera, wearing pajamas and a rain coat and wading boots. Without speaking to anyone, he climbs up on the back of a fire engine, snaps a few pictures and goes back home to bed. He will be immediately sound asleep because he hardly woke up to do his work. But his photographs will be printed and ready by five the next morning. Each will be sharp, clearly showing the pain, terror, trouble and—if it's there—the sad comedy of a late-night crackup on a lonely road."

As dedicated as he was to getting the story in pictures, pictures that often communicated so much more than the written word, Randy also had a great deal of sympathy and compassion for those he photographed. Rod Doherty, executive editor at the *Transcript*, recalls that Randy would arrive on the scene of a tragedy and get the photographs that told the story, sometimes at the cost of verbal abuse or harassment, but "minutes later he could be seen comforting those who were most immediately hurt by the series of events."

News reporters especially liked Randy and never tired of telling about their exploits with the *Transcript's* news photographer. Charles J. Hoye, a longtime *Transcript* staffer, remembers

Trabold the prankster as well as Randy the helping hand who lowered him down the ravine at Dead Man's Curve on Route 2, in order to save an overturned and leaking oil tanker rig from an explosion. Trabold's opposite number at the *Berkshire Eagle*, photographer Bill Tague, never missed an opportunity to photograph his friend in action. The last picture in this book, taken by Tague, perfectly captures Randy covering his last Williams College commencement before Randy's retirement in the fall of 1979.

Randy Trabold also took beautiful pictures. He especially delighted in the people and landscape of his beloved north county. His human portraits and landscape pictures have an almost classical dimension; they are profound, evocative, and emotionally compelling. One of my students, Kim Alice (MCLA 2000), did a study of Trabold's photographs, comparing them with art photography. "Trabold," she concluded, "always had an eye out for interesting, beautiful and unique scenes to capture with his camera. He would often emphasize form, shadow, pattern and texture, transforming the ordinary into something unique." His work was the subject of special exhibitions at the Berkshire Museum in Pittsfield in 1956 and at the Clark Art Institute in Williamstown in 1979.

Boisterous, good-natured, kind, and compassionate, Randy was loved by all. Hundreds of people flocked to see his photographs on display at MCLA in 1998 and at the Adams Free Library and Town Hall in 2001. Recalling Randy's extraordinary presence in the community, Alton Perry has provided another glimpse of the man: "In my entire life spent in this area, no person has ever approached him in popularity or in prominence. Everyone knew him, everyone loved him." Writing to Ida Trabold, Ernie Imhoff, a former *Transcript* reporter who had moved on to the *Baltimore Sun*, reflected, "There will never be another like Randy—friend, teacher, humorist, morale booster, and of course photographer and student of human nature." Maynard Leahey, in a 1980 *Transcript* article, recalled, "Going out to dine with the Trabolds, Randy and Ida, provided an insight into the range of his friendships. Every other guest, it seemed, stopped at his table to chat, and he was constantly up and bounding about the room to greet others." No wonder that Randy was selected to be grand marshall of the 1971 Northern Berkshire Fall Foliage Festival parade. Pictured on page 6 riding in the parade with his wife, Ida, and two grandchildren, Randy is truly in his element. It is fitting that his two grandchildren should be in the car of honor, for Randy's first love was children. They would gather around him wherever he went, and he would pause to listen to their stories and even take a few minutes for some playful fun. Of course, Randy especially loved to capture children on film and to shoot pictures of "kids eating spaghetti, getting a vaccination, crying, laughing and just plain being bored." In speaking of his friend Randy, Alton Perry asked the question "How do we attain success and greatness?" He answered, "We get them by the simple act of caring for our fellow man, by a kind of eternal flame of love for other people. That's how we get them—that's how Randy Trabold earned them."

Randy Trabold's Northern Berkshire County has evolved over the past five years as students in my arts management classes at the Massachusetts College of Liberal Arts have encountered his extraordinary legacy of photographs. For me, it has been a special challenge to work with these young people, many of whom initially had limited knowledge of the photographer or his subjects. The students have brought unique visual sensitivity to Randy's work. The captions they have written to accompany the photographs reflect the variety of responses the pictures have generated for them: a desire to learn more about the people and history of the area, a shared feeling of human sympathy, an appreciation for a subject's unique beauty or the photographer's artistry, a connection to the picture's innate humor, and a consequent desire to help complete the punch line.

For those of us who worked on this book project and have now brought it to completion, our hope is that you will enjoy these photographic memories of Randy's northern Berkshire County as much as we have.

—Dr. Tony Gengarelly

One

COMMUNITIES

Town and city institutions create the social and economic base that supports the northern Berkshire region's lifestyle. Over the years, northern Berkshire towns—and the only city in the area, North Adams—have experienced many changes. Some have been worked for and achieved; others have been protested and disputed. Randy Trabold used his camera to capture the towns' moments and memories before the winds of change carried them away.

In 1938 Randy Trabold left the area to work for the *New London Day*, a Connecticut-based publication, but he was soon back in the mountains and valleys of the northern Berkshires. He had returned for good to his job at the *Transcript*, recording the daily activities of the public he knew and loved. He had a passion for photojournalism and enjoyed the northern Berkshire community, especially the towns, including his "home town" North Adams, with their distinctive histories.

This late-1970s photograph provides a view of the north side of Main Street in North Adams. The Civil War statue in the immediate foreground was erected by the Ladies' Soldiers Aid Society in tribute to the town's residents who fought in the war. According to the North Adams Historical Society, "during the Civil War, the area furnished an unusually large number of soldiers in proportion to the population of the town. The people hated slavery and loved liberty and also had the courage of their convictions. The men were inspired to fight by pure patriotism." The statue was hit by a car in 1997 and had to be removed for several months while it was repaired. The Mohawk Theater is now closed, although the marquee is still there and lit every night as a nostalgic reminder of yesterday.

The trees lining the sidewalk vanish into the background as Trabold frames the vast depth and length of Main Street in North Adams. The turn-of-the-century architecture, filling the right side of this photograph, and large sidewalks make the downtown stroll a pleasant pastime for many in the northern Berkshire area.

The Roberts Company shop used to be located on Main Street in North Adams. Randy Trabold takes in the essence of the holiday shopping season with this snapshot of Nancy Mancuso, her arms filled with bag-loads of surprises. Randy probably freed his hands of the camera and lent a hand when the "photo session" was over.

Taken in 1971, this photograph shows the site of the demolished Hotel Phoenix in North Adams. The hotel was torn down after a two-alarm fire destroyed the building. Additional firefighters were called in from neighboring Williamstown and Clarksburg. It was later determined that the fire was caused by a combination of faulty wiring and years of inept repair work. The fire killed one tenant, injured another, and sent five North Adams firefighters to the hospital.

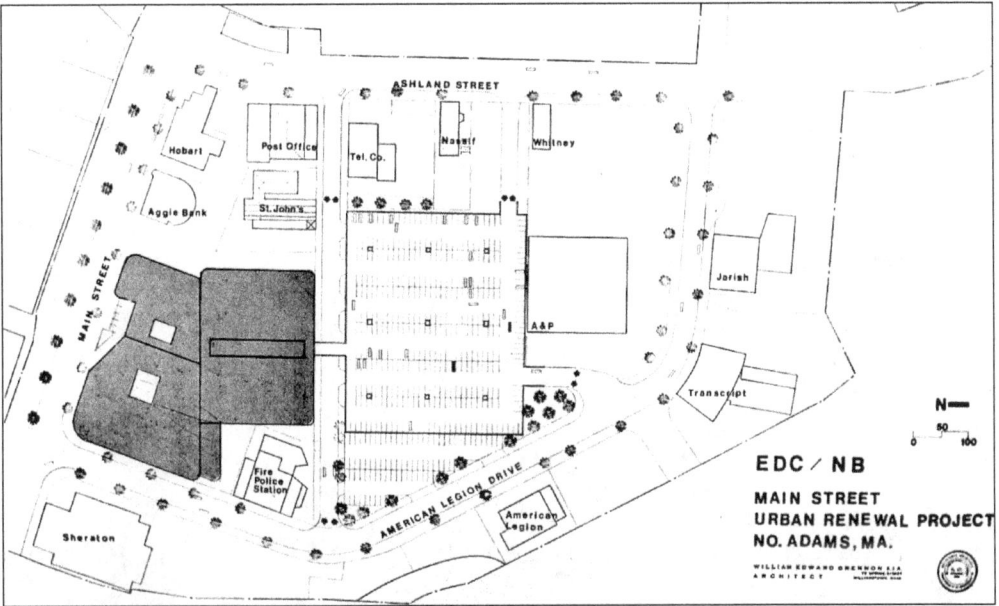

Made by architect William Edward Grennon of Williamstown, this drawing shows the plan for the North Adams urban renewal project that was undertaken from 1968 to 1974. The drawing indicates the new structures that would be built, including a new building for the *North Adams Transcript,* a shopping plaza, and a Sheraton hotel over the former site of the Hotel Phoenix.

This photograph shows the site of the Hotel Phoenix in North Adams midway through demolition. In past incarnations, the hotel was also known as the Richmond and the Wellington. In 1940, when it was known as the Wellington, the hotel suffered a severe fire that made it necessary to completely renovate the building. The hotel met the same unfortunate fate in 1971 and was torn down. A Holiday Inn now stands on the site.

The Oasis shopping plaza was constructed c. 1979 as an extension of the urban renewal project. The project required the demolition of several downtown buildings in order to construct a K-Mart and additional retail space. Several existing businesses were required to relocate. The Oasis plaza was built over what was then just an empty lot. One of its main tenants, Whitney's Package Store, had been a part of North Adams before the urban renewal project and is still there today.

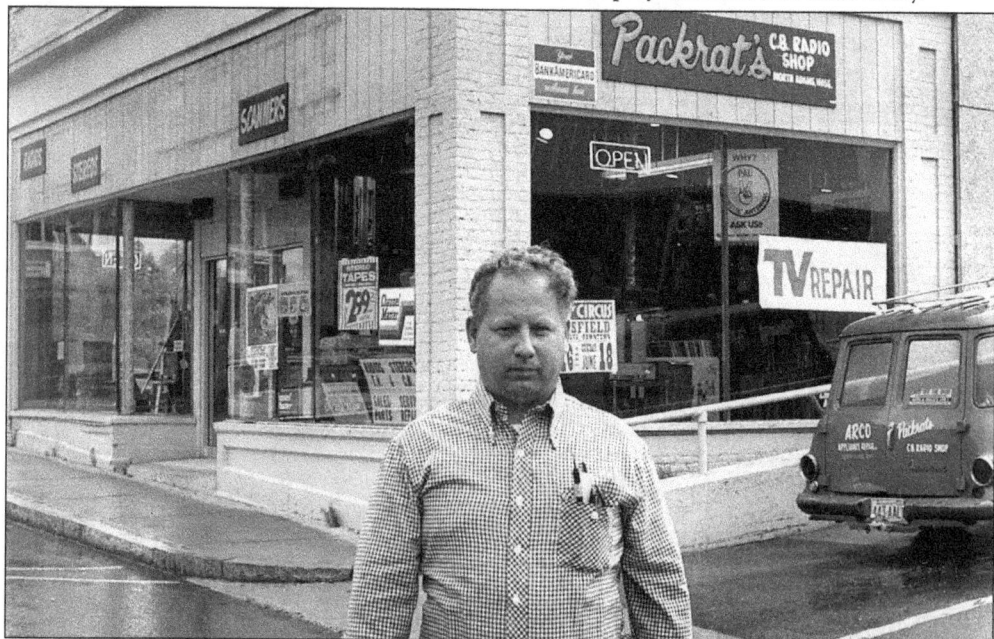

This photograph from the spring of 1978 shows Steve Patryn, former owner of Packrat's CB Radio Shop, on the corner of Main and Marshall Streets across from the new town hall in North Adams. Among other things, Packrat's was noted in the community for selling Scott Folsom records. Patryn continues to operate the Appliance Repair Company—hence, the lettering ARCO on the back of the van in the picture.

14

Located in the Maple Street Cemetery in Adams, the Quaker Meeting House was built between 1784 and 1786. The Quakers were the first settlers of Adams, and Susan B. Anthony's family worshiped here. The outside of the house was left unpainted in accord with the Quakers' belief in a simple lifestyle. The meetinghouse was used until 1842, when the Quakers more or less disappeared from the area. Other than some repairs to the slate roof and the foundation, the meetinghouse remains untouched since the time of its construction. The foreground tombstones date back as far as the late 1800s.

For many years this marble quarry in Adams was a major source of employment and revenue for the area. Now run by Specialty Minerals Inc., the quarry is still active. To the right are the step lines where the various stages of mining took place, and several of the mining company's buildings can be seen in the background.

15

These women sharpshooters trained at the Adams Rifle Club range. They are, from left to right, Patricia Verow, J. LeBeau, Gertrude Jette, Lillian Parrott, A. Stockwell, Cora Marsh, Elizabeth Hewitt, and Lillian Livsey. Trabold, photographing from down range, captures the rifle team in a more somber pose than the photograph printed in the June 5, 1942 *Transcript*. The published photograph shows the women seated and standing with their rifles pointed at the ceiling and a large American flag behind them.

On the morning of Friday, October 25, 1974, at the Adams McKinley Square monument, a pumpkin was found in President McKinley's extended hand. Willard Bard, the parks department foreman, is shown removing the pumpkin. Randy Trabold took this photograph while sharing a laugh with Bard about the ongoing pranks and gifts found in McKinley's hand over the years, including a fish.

Located at 62 Chapin Hall Drive on the Williams College campus, Chapin Hall is a large auditorium often used as a concert hall. On a Saturday morning in 1974, the Corinthian columns of Chapin Hall made the front page of the *Transcript*. Chapin Hall's architect was Ralph Adams of Cram, Goodhue, and Ferguson. Grace Hall, as it was then called, was completed in 1911–1912. The building is now named for Alfred Clark Chapin, a Williams College benefactor and former comptroller of the state of New York. On the left is Sage Hall, a student dormitory built in 1923.

In the fall of 1970, John Brooks, then associate director at the Sterling and Francine Clark Art Institute in Williamstown, inaugurated a series of tours for specific grades at the local elementary schools. A volunteer docent, Elizabeth "Liz" Scherr, is leading a tour of Marcia Gross's fourth-grade class from the Mark Hopkins School in North Adams. The students are excited to answer a question proposed to them by Scherr about the pointillist work *Madame Monnom*, created in 1900 by Théo van Rysselberghe.

Gingerbread styling in architecture was the subject matter of an article that inspired Randy Trabold to document local examples. The "Transcope" section of the September 18, 1976 *Transcript* displayed his findings. Built in 1894, this house was owned by Prof. Fred Stocking, who later sold it to Williams College. It is located at 107 Southworth Street in Williamstown. Now known as the Stocking House, this Victorian is a good example of gingerbread-styled rails, which abound on its porches and balconies. Also notable is the rounded bay window, stained glass, whimsical gold leaf in the paint, and the contrasting tower, roofline, and siding.

In the "Past in Pictures" section of the November 18, 1975 *Transcript*, Randy Trabold wrote, "Taking pictures at the Crooked Forest in Savoy was always an interesting assignment for me." The Massachusetts College of Liberal Arts Archive holds the first photograph Randy took in the Crooked Forest in 1939. In that photograph is a younger Crooked Forest with thinner timber. In this picture we see a mature Crooked Forest, with Dr. Donald Provencher standing among the trees. As noted in Trabold's 1975 caption, the forest has since gone to rot.

This was the view to the north from the top of Stafford Hill in Cheshire. In the center of the photograph is Hoosac Valley High School. The Ayer Hill Farm, now under the Farm Protection Act, is just to the right of the school. The papers in the hand of the man on the left are most likely plans for proposed units of subsidized housing for senior citizens. Although the senior-citizen housing project was never undertaken, much other development has taken place in the area since the debated project was covered in the April 17, 1978 edition of the *Transcript*.

The Green River winds its way through much of northern Berkshire County. Here it is seen flowing underneath Route 43, which connects Williamstown and Clarksburg. In this picture, taken near the south entrance to Mount Hope, Trabold captures a pristine moment that epitomizes the splendor of winter.

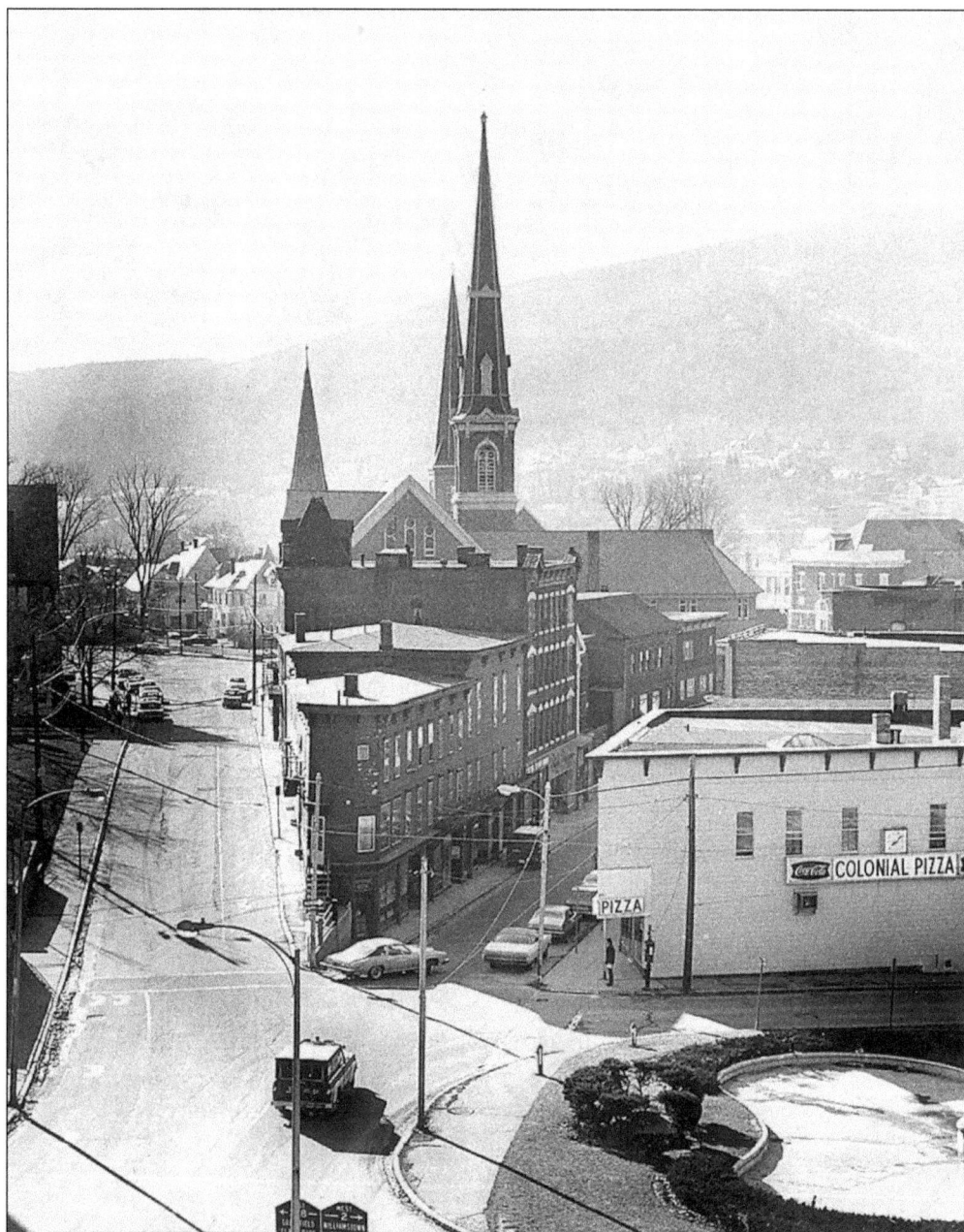

This photograph was taken in the mid-1970s from the roof of a building on the opposite side of Route 2. Although Colonial Pizza is now called Village Pizza, this quintessential downtown North Adams street corner looks much the same today as it did then. Behind the Flatiron Block, the church steeples seem to dominate the landscape, even the great sloping hills in the background, and they are still a prominent feature of North Adams that can be seen for miles around.

Two

LANDMARKS

One of the most fascinating aspects of northern Berkshire County is the many beautiful landmarks that celebrate its unique location, including the Mohawk Trail, Mount Greylock, Windsor Lake, and other famous points of interest.

Randy Trabold helped promote these landmarks through his artful photography. He visited these locations often, catching them in all seasons and as they were transformed over the years. He also recognized that they are more than beautiful sites; they are also important symbols for the area. People who visit these landmarks today will enjoy the peek into the past that Trabold's photography offers. He captured special moments and discovered extraordinary details not noticed by the untrained eye.

"It is good to think of the road as a destination within itself, not just a means to someplace far away," advised Clinton Richmond, the great-grandson of the state senator of North Adams who helped obtain the initial funding to build the Hairpin Turn, the sharp, extraordinary curve on Route 2 that, due to a quirk of cartography, begins and ends in Clarksburg. Navigating the Hairpin Turn, a familiar experience for Berkshire residents, is now a favorite stop for visitors hiking the Mohawk Trail or driving up to the Western Summit. This photograph, taken during the evening hours of a traffic jam in the 1950s, shows an enthusiastic police officer in the middle of the road, trying to keep the passage of cars under control. Trabold captures the details of the curve and how it blends with the rest of the panorama, creating an enchanting piece of artwork.

The Mohawk Trail passes through some of the most beautiful scenery in Massachusetts. Mountains surround the traveler on either side of the 63-mile highway, along with the Deerfield and Cold Rivers. Regardless of the season, there are always breathtaking views, especially near the mountaintops when approaching North Adams from the east. The trail is rich with history, including the history of its own name. There was a time when Native Americans claimed the valleys and mountains of western Massachusetts as their own. During this period a battle was fought between two rival tribes, the result of a high Mohawk chief being slain. The Mohawks took their vengeance, and with their victory came the naming of the old Native American trail in honor of them.

At 92 feet tall, the War Veterans Memorial at the summit of Mount Greylock is one of the most famous landmarks in the Berkshires. The memorial was built in 1932. A plaque near the base reads, "Erected by Massachusetts in grateful recognition of her sons and daughters. In War they were faithful even unto death." The conical granite tower with a nonoperational light at the top resembles a lighthouse. The tower is open to visitors and gives a 100-mile panoramic view of the northern Berkshires. Trabold took this photograph c. 1975, when the memorial was being restored.

23

This aerial shot depicts the renowned Sterling and Francine Clark Art Institute. The collections at the institute grew out of the private art collection that Robert Sterling Clark accumulated during his residence in Paris in 1910. He and his wife, Francine, opened the museum in Williamstown in 1955. In 1973 a new addition to the building was constructed to house the growing collection.

During the Middle Ages artists depicted religious themes on altarpieces. This altarpiece by Ugolino da Siena depicts the Virgin and child with SS. Francis, Andrew, Paul, Peter, Stephen, and Louis of Toulouse. In this graceful photograph, the curiosity in the faces of the two children and their mother is clear. The Sterling and Francine Clark Art Institute, where this piece of art resides, is especially distinguished by the depth of its collections.

24

In March 1956 Randy Trabold's photographs were on display in a one-man show at the Berkshire Museum in Pittsfield. Sponsored by the Berkshire Art Association, the show celebrated Trabold's extraordinary career to date with 24 photographs, many of them prizewinners, that covered the spectrum of his subjects, from spot news pictures to landscape and human-interest features.

Sterling Clark, Francine Clark, and the first director of the Clark Art Institute, Peter Guille, are shown here in the early days of the museum. Guille, a flamboyant personality, successfully promoted the new museum until his retirement in 1966. Another former Clark Art Institute director, David Brooke, described the Clarks' collection as a very personal one and observed that Sterling Clark was a person who loathed publicity. The Clarks and Peter Guille apparently complemented each other very well.

25

What attracts the viewer to this picture is the officer standing rigid yet calm in the foreground. In the background, there seems to be a small commotion around the overturned truck that has just blocked the Mohawk Trail. The Mohawk Trail stretches from the Massachusetts–New York line to Millers Falls on the Connecticut River. It is also known as the 63-mile east-west highway. Over the years the Mohawk Trail has been widened and graded and now bears heavy traffic that increases the occurrence of vehicle accidents.

One of the things that makes the Mohawk Trail so popular is the beauty of the views from the top of the mountains. At Whitcomb Summit, the highest on the trail at 2,240 feet, four states are visible. In the winter the Mohawk Trail can be a dangerous place, especially for drivers. Whitcomb Summit is in the town of Florida, ironically so-named because it has the coldest temperatures in Massachusetts. Trabold's sense of humor comes alive in this picture, as the prospect of tourists stopping to buy souvenirs in this weather and season is highly unlikely.

The Hoosac Tunnel has continued to be a popular spot in the Berkshires, although the tunnel is no longer used for passenger trains. The tunnel runs 4.8 miles underneath the Berkshire Mountain range. It took 22 years to complete, using all of the most modern technology of the 19th century. The tunnel made it possible to ship freight directly from Boston to New York and also increased tourism in the area. It opened for the first freight train on April 5, 1875.

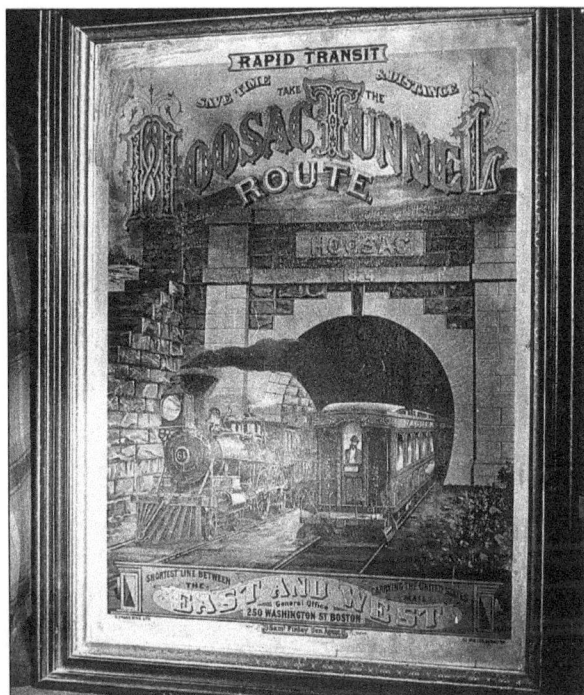

This Trabold photograph of the Western Portal of the Hoosac Tunnel shows one of the Berkshires' most fascinating and historic landmarks. The building of the Hoosac Tunnel was one of the biggest undertakings of the 19th century in the northeastern United States. Thousands of men worked on the construction of the tunnel using dangerous explosives and machines.

This photograph, taken by Randy Trabold on the western side of Whitcomb Summit on the Mohawk Trail, captures a bronze elk erected in June 1923. The elk is dedicated to all members of the Elks brotherhood who lost their lives in World War I. Is that an ocean rippling behind the elk and the souvenir shop in the midst of the Berkshire Mountains? A closer investigation

reveals that it is not an ocean of water but a sea of clouds caught below the summit of the mountain. It is such moments that transcend the typical beauty of the Berkshires and transform them into a magical realm. Trabold's talent for seeing the extraordinary in the ordinary made him into the artist he was.

One of the most popular seasons in the northern Berkshires is the fall. During this time the roads are clogged with cars featuring out-of-state license plates. On the Mohawk Trail, leaf peepers stop at shops that dot the sides of the road. One such place is the Wigwam Gift Shop on the Western Summit. It sells souvenirs of the area, and its setting provides one of the best views of the northern Berkshires.

From the summit of Mount Greylock, five states are visible in the distance and the surrounding towns of Adams, North Adams, and Williamstown can also be seen. The famous Appalachian Trail runs through the area. Here Trabold captures the feeling of having hiked to the summit, as the viewer can look down into the minuscule town of Adams through the art of his photography. The foreground tree suggests the compositional formula of 19th-century landscape artists such as Thomas Cole.

In the northern Berkshires, winter is a time of icicles, snow, freezing temperatures, and beautiful scenery. This is apparent throughout Randy Trabold's body of work, including this photograph of a picnic area off the Mohawk Trail. The pitched roofs of the enclosures are lined with long icicles reflecting the winter light.

Driving on the Mohawk Trail in winter can be an unforgettable experience. The rock outcroppings that shape the highway near the Hairpin Turn become enclosed by layers of ice, as this photograph depicts. Beautiful sheets of crystallized ice blaze with reflections on sunny days.

Throughout the north county are numerous kinds of cemeteries, ranging from church-affiliated ones to city and town cemeteries, small family plots, and sites that have long been neglected. Randy Trabold might have paused to consider that three beautiful, blooming elm trees once grew in the middle of this place, their roots intertwined with the city's past generations. The three trees now provide the viewer's focal point and line up one of the narrow roads that intersect the Hillside Cemetery, shown here.

Nestled in a bed of hills, underneath the sunny, blue skies, lies this panoramic snapshot of one of several cemeteries located in the northern Berkshires. While driving around the Adams and North Adams regions, do not be surprised if you encounter various stores that have information about bronze cemetery markers, memorial parks, cemetery equipment and supplies, cemetery lot brokers, maintenance and service for cemeteries, pet cemeteries, and headstone makers.

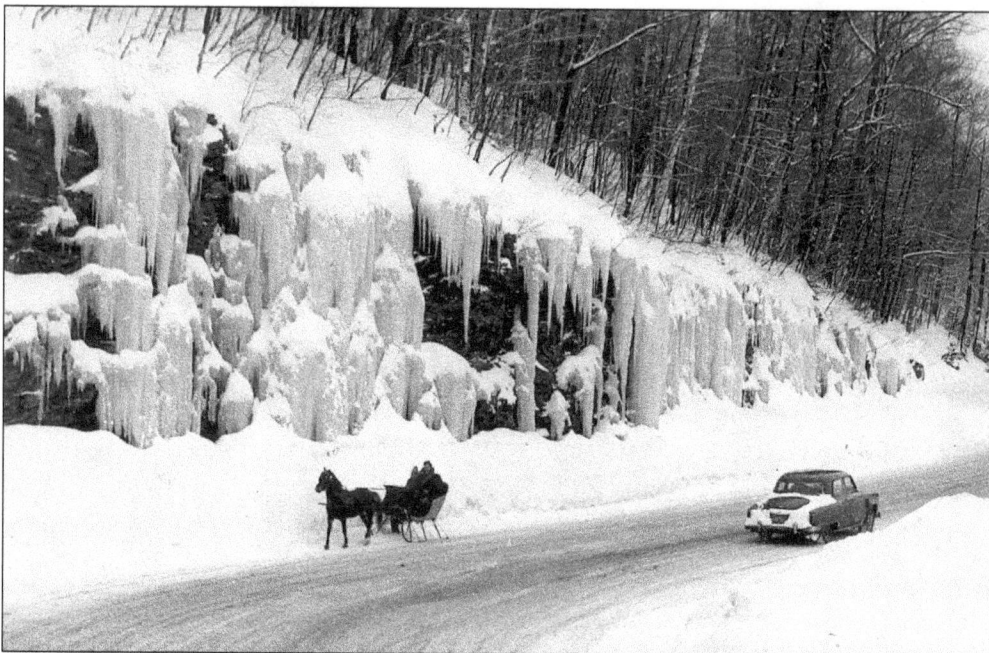

A drive in the country means two very separate things for the travelers in this photograph. On one side of the highway, an automobile climbs the icy mountain, slowly making its way around the 180-degree turn, and, on the other, a horse and sleigh glide through the snow. The horse and sleigh belonged to Adolph Heidemann Jr. from Clarksburg, and the viewer can almost imagine bells jingling from harnesses and the passengers' cheeks red from the cold.

One of Randy Trabold's favorite landmarks to photograph was Mount Greylock State Park, opened to the public in 1898. The winter months provide some of the most brilliant views of the landscape. The snow changes the viewer's perception of the Berkshires and creates almost otherworldly sights. The man caught in this photograph was one of Trabold's friends, Anthony Talarico, who appears in many of the photographer's pictures of Mount Greylock.

Apparently no cats are allowed in St. John's Episcopal Church on Summer Street in North Adams. Trabold captures the irony of the moment in this light-hearted jab at the church's welcoming sign on the doors.

Many say Mount Greylock holds a special power. During the 1950s and 1960s, the Mount Greylock Protective Association was developed to defeat the plan of ambitious entrepreneurs and politicians who wanted to construct parking lots and ski resorts on top of the mountain. The North Adams annual report for that year indicates that these tractors were working to open a path to the mountain, before conservationists mobilized to restrict development.

This photograph transforms traffic rounding the Hairpin Turn into an artistic image. Trabold used a time-exposure technique to blur the vehicles' headlights into a seemingly solid line. In order to get this shot, the photographer would have opened and shut the shutter of the camera by hand or would have used a mechanism other than the automatic operation of the shutter. It is a process that makes the end photograph show what the natural eye can only imagine.

Three

THE FAMILY OF MAN

The family of man is exactly what has been captured in Randy Trabold's portraits. These photographs provide an account of the people who have lived in northern Berkshire County. These pictures are their moments and memories, their emotions and actions captured by the lens of a camera and the eye of a photographer. They portray people of all ages and backgrounds. They display carefree moments and moments that truly touch the heart. The photographs are not only pictures of lives but windows into them. Each face on film portrays not only part of the northern Berkshire family but the human spirit itself.

According to a 1979 citation from Massachusetts College of Liberal Arts, "Randy always sees you, whether you're the biggest or the littlest." This statement certainly describes Trabold as a person and a photographer. He was out to cover the biggest news stories, but he also had a talent and desire to capture everyday life. He had a special love of photographing children and did so often. In his 44 years as a photographer for the *Transcript*, Trabold recorded several generations of people on film. He was invited into their homes, and his photographs now hang on many people's walls as examples of Randy's talent and the memories that his pictures helped preserve.

Robert John LaBombard Jr. has not been able to escape this photograph. It has followed him all of his life. People call to interview him and to ask whether they can take his picture alongside this award-winning photograph Trabold shot on September 6, 1961. It was taken on LaBombard's first day of school at St. Joseph's Catholic School in North Adams. LaBombard recalls that his teacher's name was Sister St. Agnes but does not remember seeing the photographer: "I'm sure he was just another adult to me. I was yawning, and he caught it. The bow tie was mom's idea." LaBombard did not ever meet Randy Trabold, but the photographer did have an impact on his life, as he will be long remembered as the archetypical child who found school a bore.

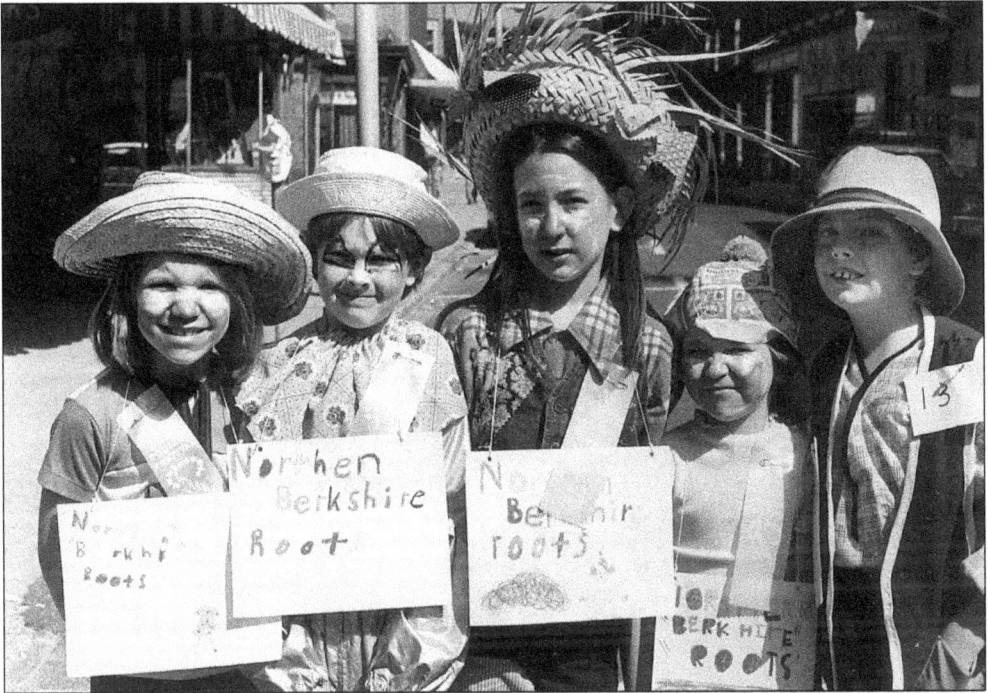

The children pictured here in costume are participants in the Children's Parade at the 1978 Fall Foliage Festival in North Adams. They are, from left to right, Erin O'Brien, Jamie Nimmons, Jen Gwozdz, Colleen O'Brien, and Michelle Richard. The theme for the 1978 festival was "Northern Berkshire Roots."

In 1978 Randy Trabold and his wife, Ida, accompanied 40 other people from the Massachusetts College of Liberal Arts Alumni Association on a trip to Costa Rica. This young newsboy is sitting on a street in San José, the capital of the country. In his caption for this photograph, Trabold wrote, "The newspaper, obviously, is not *The Transcript*."

There may have been snow on the ground and a nip in the air, but it did not hinder Nick Costa from posing for Randy. Costa was department commander of Local 996 Military Order of the Cootie. (The name originated from the bed bugs the American soldiers encountered in the trenches during World War I.) He served in the army in Europe during World War II and received a Purple Heart. Besides being a member of the Veterans of Foreign Wars, Costa was a member of the American Legion, Post 125, in North Adams.

Randy Trabold was a talented photographer capable of capturing the human spirit. In this photograph he has done just that, along with a little bit of nationalistic pride. Pictured here is Tammy Therrien at age 17 holding an American flag crocheted by her mother in honor of the national bicentennial. Tammy attended McCann Technical School in North Adams. About Trabold she says, "He was a very nice, personable, popular man. He was the best photographer North Adams ever had."

North Adams was a major hub of rail transportation in 1935, the year Arthur L. Cary Jr. started working as a linesman for the Boston and Maine Railroad. One of his earliest duties was to recharge the electric locomotives that ran seven miles from the Hoosac Tunnel to North Adams. Cary was on call all hours of the day and night. If there was an ice storm on the Mohawk Trail, he was there to put the line back up. When the price of copper was high, he was frequently called to replace the lines after scavengers cut the wires for scrap. Sometimes the problem was as simple as squirrels eating the insulation off the wires. Cary was there when they ran the overhead electric lines through the tunnel and again when they ripped them out. Here, at age 60, he is about to retire after 43 years on the job.

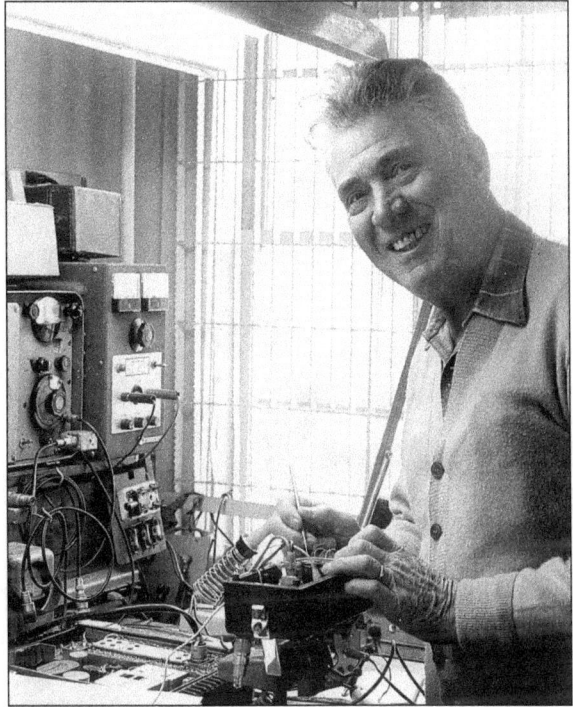

When the United States celebrated the 200th anniversary of its independence, North Adams jumped on the bandwagon. In the background are Abraham Lincoln and Colonial American look-alikes. In the foreground George Bisacca prances gallantly on his steed. Bisacca epitomizes the story of the American dream. He grew up as an orphan in Italy. When he got older, he immigrated to the United States. In 1946 he purchased a mansion in Lenox, originally owned by multimillionaire Harris Fahnestock, and converted the estate into the Eastover resort. With the horse, parade route, and buildings at three-quarter view, Bisacca looks the photographer straight in the face. The trick of shooting up at the subject allowed Trabold to portray his subject as "larger than life."

The clock in the tower of the former Sprague Electric Company used to be wound by hand, before the conversion to electricity. After graduating from Hoosac Valley High School in 1972, Mark Gajda went to work for Sprague Electric. In the late 1970s, when Randy took this picture, Mark had been assigned the exclusive duty of repairing the company's clock tower. This picture was a "set up" (Mark let it slip!), as Randy would sometimes create.

William T. Isherwood of North Adams stands before the 80-foot clock tower located on the 13-acre span of what used to be the home of the Sprague Electric Company. As keeper of the clock, Isherwood would scale the steep stairs of the tower to wind the clock twice weekly before its conversion to electricity. Isherwood was an electrician at the company for 34 years. Pictured here after his retirement, he was one of the 4,200 people employed by Sprague in North Adams. This clock, with its bells, set the rhythm of the workday in North Adams beginning in 1895, ringing every quarter-hour. It was silenced for several years after Sprague Electric vacated the premises in 1986 but was brought back to life with the opening of the Massachusetts Museum of Contemporary Art on the site in 1998.

Tony Trimarchi was a field director for the James Hunter Machine Company. His job entailed assembling machinery all over Europe, South America, Mexico, Canada, and the United States. Randy Trabold took this picture in the late 1970s, after Trimarchi had returned from a trip to Tehran, Iran, to install equipment. Upon arriving at his hotel in Tehran, he found out that it had been blown up the day before. He turned around and took the next flight he could find back to the United States. The map you see here shows the places Trimarchi had traveled to and the destination of the quickest trip of his life.

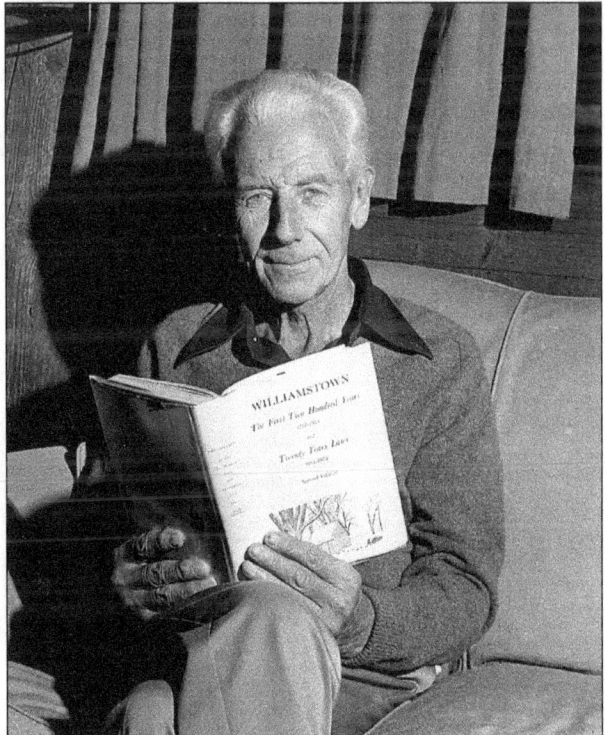

In this photograph, Trabold has captured a man and his work. Prof. Robert Romano Ravi Brooks sits before the photographer with his book in hand, *Williamstown: The First Two Hundred Years and Twenty Years Later*. Brooks was editor of this book, which was written as part of the bicentennial celebration. The text was completed in a mere six months, and Wiliamstown residents produced every part of it except for the volume's bindings. Brooks also wrote several chapters of the text. An accomplished writer, he served as chairman of the Bicentennial Historical Committee in Williamstown and spent a term as the cultural attaché of the American embassy in New Delhi.

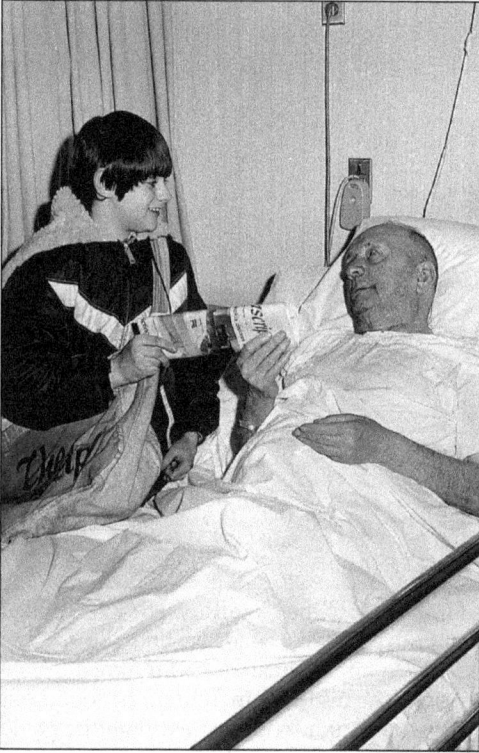

Another winter snowstorm had hit the Berkshires in early February 1978, but that did not keep 12-year-old Eric St. Cyr from delivering the *Transcript*. How lucky that was for one subscriber, Clinton Germain, who had fallen in his apartment and had been unable to move or get up for three days. St. Cyr was putting the paper between the outer and inner door of Germain's apartment when he heard a faint "Wait!" Opening the inner door, he found the elderly man on the floor and alerted a neighbor to summon help. Germain survived because of the young St. Cyr, who received a plaque for his "uncommon presence of mind and humane efforts" from the *Transcript* and a Meritorious Award for Outstanding Citizenship from the American Legion. Randy Trabold took this picture of St. Cyr delivering the *Transcript* to Germain in the hospital. This photograph went all over the country via the Associated Press.

Steve (left) and Walt Mazza lived at 55 River Street in North Adams, a location that appeared not in *Better Homes and Gardens* but in the collection of Randy Trabold. The Mazzas often rescued stray animals from trees or the Hoosac River. The creatures usually wound up living in the backyard of the apartment building. There was always a lack of food for the strays, and grooming was unheard of. The boys' attire here is the way they looked most of the time. Randy captured life as he saw it.

44

As always, summertime brings boys out to work on construction projects. Seen here is the multilayered tree house fabricated in the late 1960s on the property of Dixon Daniels of Adams. There is a lot more happening here than painting and hammering. Daniels owned the L.L. Brown Paper Company, located in Adams. The wood for the tower came from old lumber used for shipping at the mill and would get carted home in a dump truck. The pedals of the truck had been modified so that the young craftsmen could move supplies on site. "Skipper" Daniels, Dixon's son, can be seen in the upper left with striped pants and paint brush. This was just one of the many stages of evolution for the tree house and the boys. The structure eventually became seven stories high. As the lads turned into teenagers, the "clubhouse" was moved to a barn, also on Daniels's property. Interests turned to partying and racing motorcycles, and the group became known as the Barn Boys.

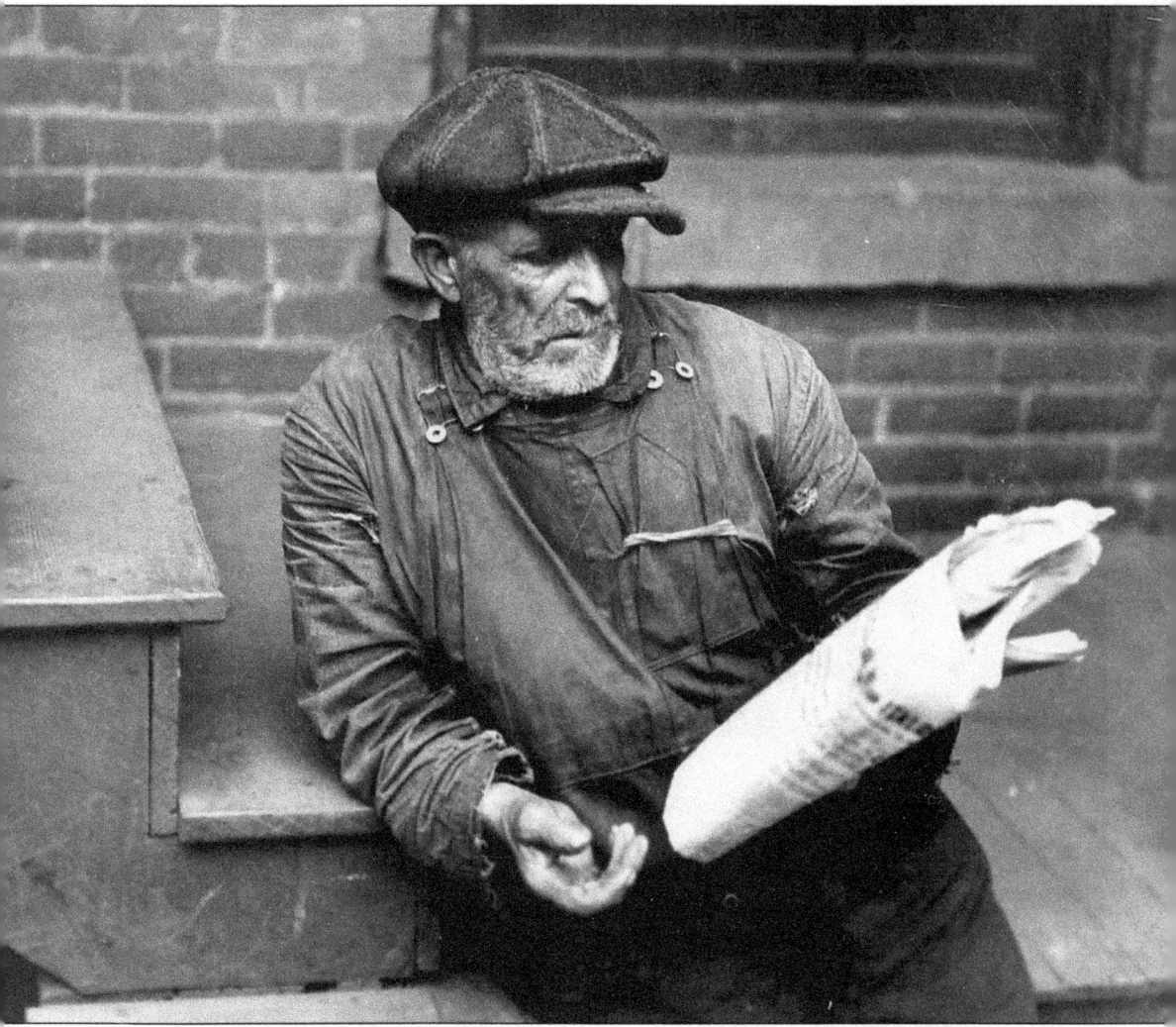

This man reading a newspaper may have been asked to pose by Trabold, or he may have just been sitting down on the stairs to catch up on the day's events. At first the viewer wants to know his name, to know what the headlines were on this day, but it begins to seem unimportant. As the viewer observes an ordinary person doing something we all do every day, something remarkable has been captured on film. His face and hands tell us a story about him and about ourselves.

Here Trabold has captured Mrs. Frank Maruco in a dramatic portrait of powerful emotion. Trabold focuses on certain qualities of his subject in order to capture her grief. Her face, hands, and rosary are lit from the right. With these highlights, we can see the emotion across her face and also the way her hands are clasped around her rosary. These lighted objects contrast with her dark clothing and with the dark buildings behind her, drawing attention to the hands and face. The sharp angles of the buildings in the background also contrast with the brilliant sky to accentuate the figure. Trabold often used the elements of photography in an artistic manner in order to convey feeling.

As icicles make a romantic backdrop, Walter and Susan Getchell dance at the annual Snow Ball, hosted by the Williamstown Boys' Club. Some 200 people turned out for the ball on February 12, 1978. The *Transcript* described the event: "Dressed in their finery, municipal officials and townspeople dropped their daily conservative businesslike look and let their hair down." This certainly included the Getchells. They were two of many who attended the ball, at which there was hardly any room on the dance floor for those dancing to the Williams College Jazz Ensemble's big-band sound. Susan Getchell was a faculty member for 19 years at what was then North Adams State College, and Walter Getchell was a musician and the band director at Mount Greylock High School.

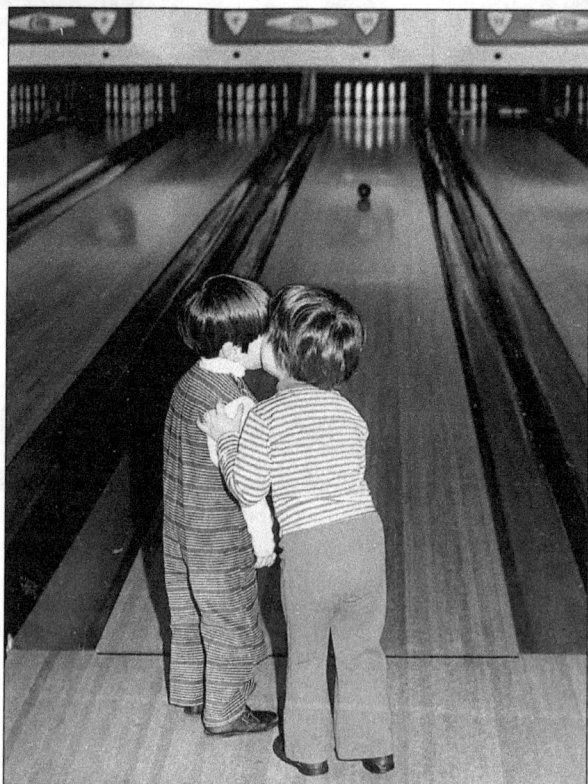

Lori Cain and a friend at Valley Park Lanes in North Adams are caught in a wonderful Trabold candid moment with children.

On a lazy summer day in 1975, William Levesque reclines under his idea of an air conditioner. This photograph was taken in North Adams at the Wheel Estates Trailer Park. William Levesque was known in the area as Bill Bishop, a popular meat cutter. He spoke French fluently and was especially well known by the French-speaking population. He worked at the A & P supermarket in North Adams and at Colonial Village in Williamstown. The creative ice cube hanging above him was fashioned by his son Bob, who worked at the Cornish Wire Company in Williamstown. Levesque's son Buster commented, "Little did he know when he was complaining about posing for this picture that his great great-grandchildren would be able to see it published."

Robert Cambell and his dog Brownie were found hitchhiking on the Mohawk Trail *c*. 1953. The shopping bag contains a change of clothes and meat for the dog. Later, when police picked him up, Cambell showed them his diary, in which he had recorded the beatings his father had given to him. It gave details of the dates of the beatings, the type of violence he had been the victim of, and his father's unstable state of mind. After questioning the boy, the police returned him to his parents, but the dog was left behind. Trabold makes a powerful comment here through his astute recognition of the boy's plight, which apparently went unheeded by the police.

Trabold's photographs were known for portraying the best of times and the worst of times and for covering things from hard-breaking news to events from everyday life. He especially enjoyed photographing children. In this photograph he has accomplished all of these things. The expressions on the children's faces here suggest, as do their dress and poses, that they have recently experienced a serious, even sad event. One of the older children is protectively guarding her younger sibling. The youngest girl in the forefront is wearing slippers instead of shoes, and her brother behind her is wrapped in a blanket. These observations and the note written by Trabold on the reverse side of the photograph, which reads "a heroine," suggest that the children may have been victims of a house fire.

The child, unaware of the photographer's presence, his cotton candy partially eaten, lifts his sweater to wipe his mouth, and the moment is captured. This shot is a wonderful example of Trabold's sensitivity to the individual moment and his talent for bringing human interest to visual images.

Four

LANDSCAPES

Northern Berkshire County has always been recognized and appreciated for the beauty of its landscape. Whether looking over the view that inspired Herman Melville or hiking past a stone etched with the words of Henry David Thoreau, there is much to appreciate. This area was very special to Randy Trabold, as the landscape of the Berkshire region gave him many opportunities to pursue the more artistic side of his trade. Trabold's personal collection of landscape shots closely rivals the number of images that he took in 44 years of working for the *North Adams Transcript*.

Serenity reigns over this winter scene in the absence of usually strong seasonal winds in the Berkshires. The composition is focused in such a way that it seems as if Trabold arranged the scene himself. The branches of the many trees form a single arc. The large stone lying in the foreground helps to ground the subject. The hills roll back on each side, revealing a magnificent backdrop that completes the composition. This mastery of compositional technique is what makes Randy Trabold such a celebrated photographer.

The waters of Cheshire Lake curl around the shores along the Berkshire Mountains between Cheshire and Lanesboro. The silence of the morning remains unbroken, as many residents have yet to begin their day. The early morning drive to work, however, provides travelers on Route 8 with a beautiful background for their commute.

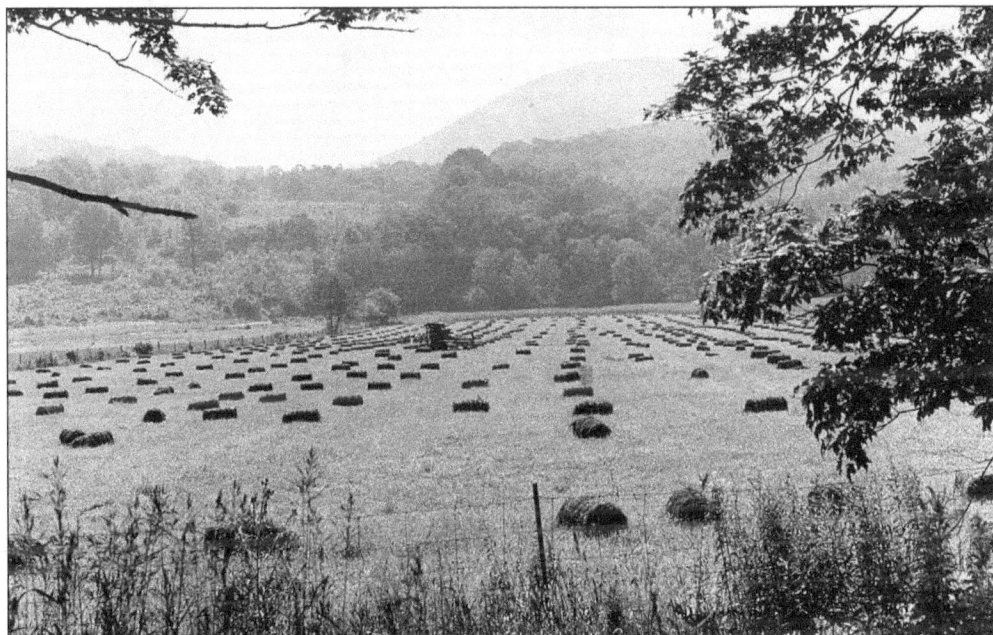

This photograph features rows of baled hay, running directly outward from the viewer's perspective and into the distance. Trees frame the image on the top and sides, and a fence and grass frame the bottom. There is a great contrast between the dark shadows of the location from which Randy Trabold took the photograph and the bright sunlit hay field. During his career, Trabold spent much time artfully capturing the farmland of Berkshire County.

This photograph depicts one of the many small farms that used to dot the area around North Adams. After completion of the Hoosac Tunnel, the area changed from a predominantly farming community to a more diversified economy.

This lone farm sits in a sublime stretch of land along the Berkshire Mountain range. Trabold captures the pastoral ideal, the life lived close to nature, celebrated by the region's painters since the early 19th century.

In this picture of Windsor Lake in North Adams, Trabold uses a high contrast of shadow and light to accentuate even the most routine of scenes. The dark silhouettes of the trees help draw the pond closer to the foreground as well as dim the glare from sunlight. The bright sun shining on the ice-covered branches complements the shadows, seemingly adding a little color to the black-and-white composition.

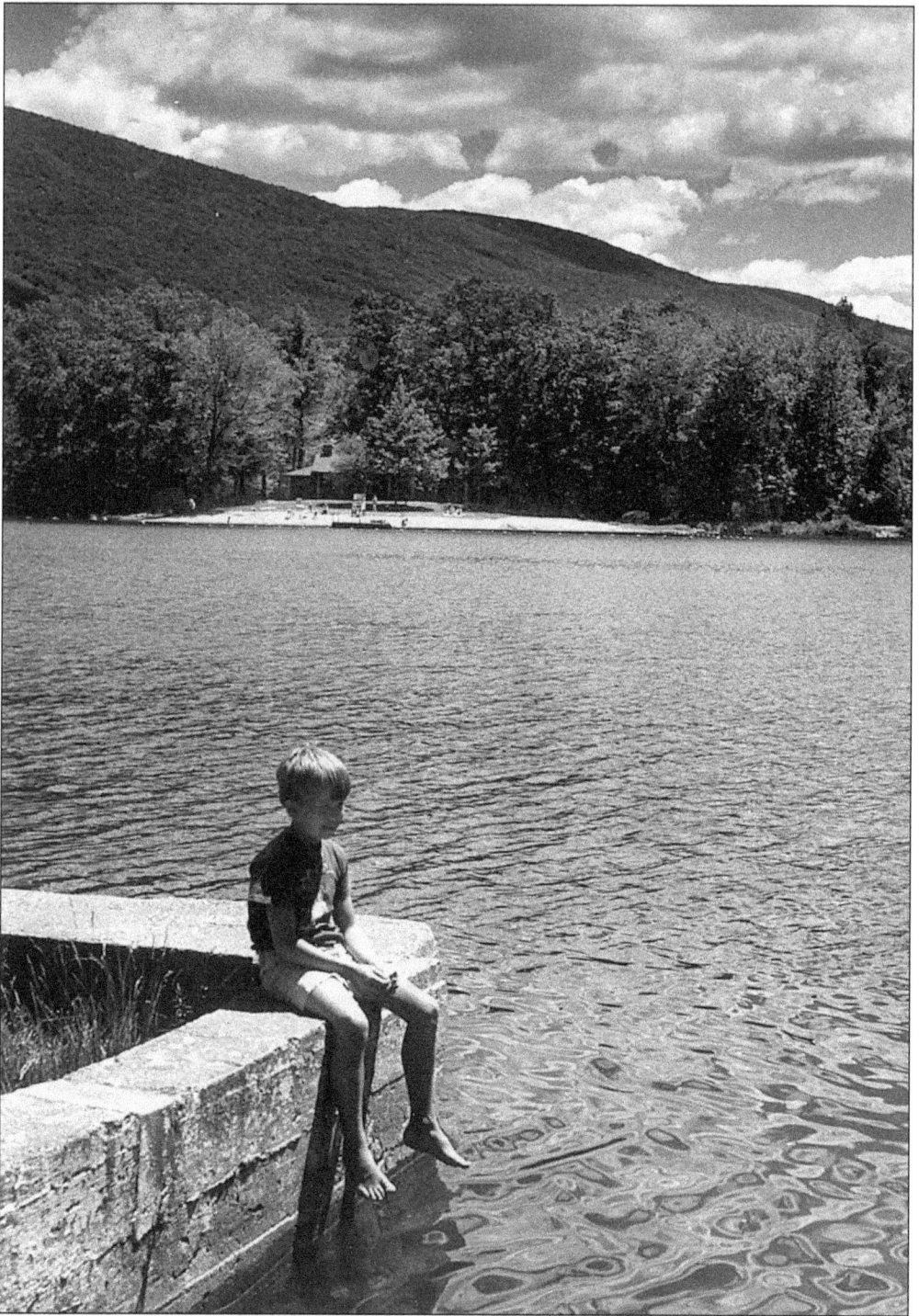

Sitting on a ledge along the shore of Cheshire Lake in Cheshire, this young boy enjoys the tranquility of the fading summer day. The waves are calm, a rarity since the harbor is a busy one. A bicycle path now circles the lake, and it is a favorite spot for many local social and sporting events.

Farming in Berkshire County continues to be a major source of economic prosperity. Over 12 percent of the state's farmland is located here. As of 1997, there were a total of 387 farms covering 62,833 acres and taking in $21 million in farm products. Among the products generated are greenhouse and nursery plants along with hay, silage, and vegetables, but the major source of agricultural income is from dairy farming.

This photograph features Mount Greylock in the background. During the 19th century, the mountain was subject to many foresting and mining operations. Local residents decided to take action to preserve Mount Greylock, and the Greylock Park Association was formed in 1885. The group purchased 400 acres. Today more than 12,500 acres of land have been preserved. The protected land is spread over six towns in Berkshire County and features many Great Depression–era buildings. The most distinctive and famous feature of the mountain is the tower that makes Greylock instantly recognizable.

Many schools can boast about their impressive sports facilities, but none can truly compare to the view that awaits the athletes at Drury High School in North Adams. With the Berkshire Mountains as a backdrop and downtown North Adams nestled just below, competitors are treated to a magnificent setting for their contests on the field. By using a sharp contrast between the shadows surrounding the roadway and the brightness of the morning, Randy Trabold draws our attention to the view of the city.

The sun sets behind the mountains overlooking Adams. The shops and diners along Main Street will soon be closed for the evening. From the benches lining the park in the town center, any onlooker who takes the time to stop will be treated to a stunning sunset over the mountains.

Many surprises are just around the corners on Route 8 in the Berkshires. The roads that circle the mountains are lined with frequent scenic rest areas, some obvious to passing motorists and some—like this one—not so obvious. Views such as this are a worthwhile reward for anyone willing to take the time to search them out.

Windsor Lake, also known as Fish Pond, is a very popular fishing spot in North Adams. The surrounding thicket of trees helps retain the peaceful seclusion that makes this a perfect spot for anglers.

This photograph of Demers' Farm, located on Wood Road in Clarksburg, features two silos used for storing grain. According to a local Williamstown farmer, Dan Galusha, "You just don't see many silos anymore." Today silos have been replaced by a two- or three-sided, open shoebox-shaped cement structure that will store more firmly packed ensilage.

Randy Trabold captures a skier beginning a descent of Mount Greylock, the highest summit in Massachusetts. The Greylock Summit Memorial Lighthouse serves as a starting point for our athlete's nearly 3,500-foot run. But thrill seekers are not permitted to feel the rush of this nearly 1-mile adventure because Mount Greylock is not open for commercial skiing. Or perhaps this man is merely a model placed into Trabold's composition in order to create a finished piece. Either way, Randy Trabold masterfully captures the excitement and magnificence that lies on top of Mount Greylock.

Many of today's working Berkshires farms were originally cleared by settlers who had come to the area for lumbering. The rivers that cut through the valleys of northern Berkshire County have provided farmers with irrigated water and have served as sources of power for mills and factories.

The Boston and Maine freight line traveled from Boston to all points west and north to Maine. This freight service carried coal and other goods through the Hoosac Tunnel to the northern Berkshire area. This picture artfully shows the grandeur of the train and the relentless power of industrial transportation. Trabold makes us reflect here about the impact of industrial technology on the rural landscape. Coming out of the smoke of industry, the train brings material progress but at a cost to the land.

North Adams quickly evolved from a small logging and farming community into a major industrial center in a relatively short time during the second half of the 19th century. The city was in an advantageous location for industry because of its many waterways, and the main influence on its rapid development was the building of the Hoosac Tunnel. Many developers and industries then began looking to the North Adams area as a place of major business opportunity.

This photograph offers an aerial view of Windsor Lake. The 17-acre man-made lake is mostly owned by the city of North Adams. It is located approximately a half-mile east of Route 8. Its average depth is 8 feet, with its deepest point being 19 feet. A gravel boat ramp was built on the lake's northern cove for launching canoes, and there are many swimming and fishing areas located along the lake's shores.

During its prime, North Adams was a center for railroad traffic. The city was home to two different railroads—the Bangor and Aroostook and the Boston and Maine. Tracks can be seen throughout the city. This photograph features a dual set of tracks, and around this area one can often see two passing trains. Spectators can get a good look at the trains from the city's many footbridges.

Five

HARD-BREAKING NEWS

Randy Trabold dedicated his life to capturing the joys and sorrows of the people living in Berkshire County. Influenced by his father, who had a photography studio in North Adams, Randy wanted to be a photographer from the time he was a child. Day or night, he would rush to the scene of a newsworthy incident to record what was happening on film. There was friendly competition with other news photographers in Berkshire County, as they were all anxious to get the best picture. Randy's edge was that he had a great eye for the perfect shot and was very loyal to his community.

This chapter is dedicated to Randy's life as a news photographer. It shows how he recorded the large as well as the small moments in northern Berkshire history that needed to be remembered. As a photojournalist, he not only captured the moment but also gave us a narrative about what was happening. When photographing fires, floods, and accidents, Randy always found a powerful way to depict them without sensationalizing. In this chapter are many examples of Randy's talent as a news photographer and his deeply compassionate nature.

Randy Trabold caught the bitter moments of life in a very compelling way. He took this prizewinning spot news photograph on May 22, 1959, at a Stamford, Vermont fire that destroyed the home of Stanley Sumner. Published the following day, it shows Mae Sumner holding her five-month-old son, Kirk, and her pet kitten, which she had snatched from the fire, as the house burns in the background.

Robert C. Sprague Jr. of Williamstown was a lover of antique cars. He had a wonderful collection that took years to acquire. In the summer of 1974, Sprague decided to open up his barn and allow the public to view the collection. His exhibitions were a great success, until June 22, when kerosene dripping from a fuel tank accidentally ignited. The barn and many irreplaceable automobiles were destroyed. Lost in the fire were the only two 1906 Model H Cadillacs known to be in existence, as well as a 1902 Wheeler, the first model off the production line. A 1909 Stevens Duryea XXX and a 1925 Silver Ghost Rolls Royce were badly damaged but restorable.

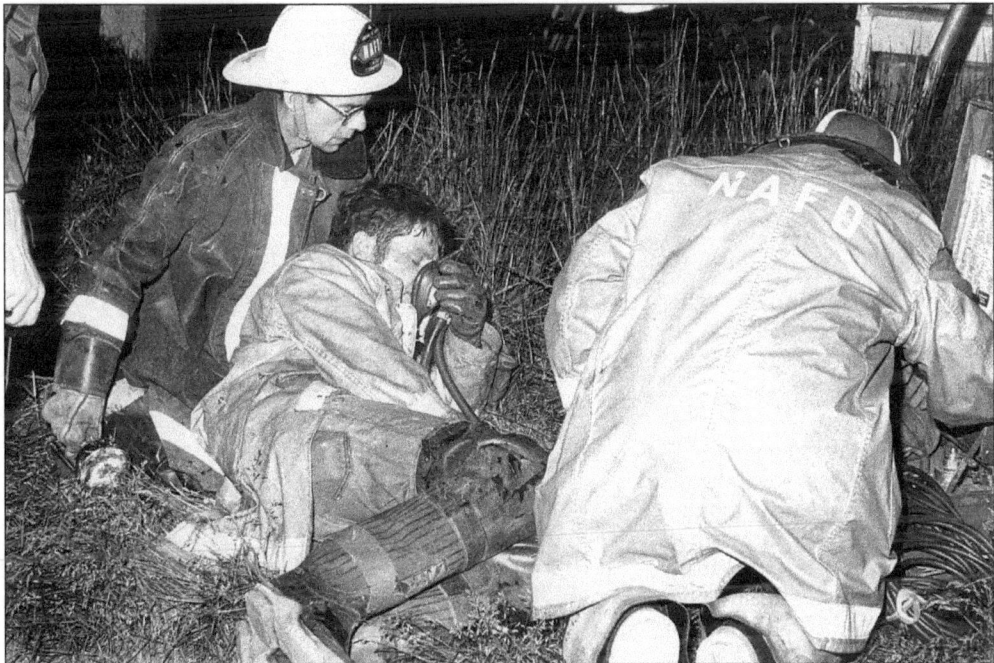

Randy Trabold used photography the way a reporter used words to tell people what was going on. In this picture he shows the team effort of the North Adams Fire Department. On the left is John Law, the wire inspector, giving oxygen to Anthony Sacco, overcome by smoke and exhaustion while battling a blazing fire.

National Guard Sgt. Ralph Parmenter and police patrolmen Howard Bartlett and Euclide Gagner are shown carrying a terrified Mrs. Albright from her home on River Street during the Hurricane of 1938. The men rushed into her house to carry her to safety just minutes before the floodwaters began to rush in.

Even in the wake of a great regional disaster, such as the flood of 1950, Trabold always found a way to get a human-interest (in this case, animal-interest) story. While floodwaters rise around her house, Mildred Mahoney of 19 Washington Avenue has one concern: her dog Whitey. Whitey is afraid of the water and does not want to leave his house. His owner tries to move him to safety.

70

After a week of torrential rains and a hurricane pelted New England, the Hoosac River flooded its banks and swamped much of North Adams on September 21, 1938. Brooklyn Street, shown here, was completely torn up and its sidewalks destroyed. Trabold covered the story and recalled that "staffers worked through the night, writing copy by the light of lanterns, flashlights and candles. The doorways to the *Transcript* building were sandbagged to keep the water away from the press, and electricity was finally hooked up sufficiently to print an early morning extra."

Randy Trabold was always on the lookout for the most interesting and unusual situations to photograph. Several workers watch as this derailed train car is lowered safely into the river.

Even in the wake of disaster, Randy Trabold found intriguing ways to comment on the human situation. This little boy, astonished, stares at the partially submerged train car. Randy catches the natural fascination human beings have with the extraordinary.

This fire, blazing through the night into the morning of October 20, 1953, caused over $150,000 in damage and destroyed the warehouse and sales room at the Dibble Lumber Yard, along with several nearby offices and a house. The fire was discovered early in the morning as it tore through the roof of the warehouse. Engine 1 from the North Adams Fire Department was on duty in another part of town and did not arrive until 45 minutes later. Other engines were already on the scene when Engine 1 arrived, but it was the only fire truck that could access the main water supply from the Hoosac River. The firemen had things under control by 8:00 a.m., but the cause of the fire was never determined.

The gentleman pictured here was fortunate not to have injured himself badly, and he allowed Randy to take this posed photograph. The facial expression portrays the gravity of the man's situation and perhaps the impact this accident has had on his life.

During most of the 20th century, the Capitol Theatre was a popular entertainment spot. One evening in the early 1950s, *Judge Hardy and Son*, starring Mickey Rooney and Lewis Stone, was the featured picture at the Capitol. A late-night calamity occurred when the fourth floor

of the building caught fire spontaneously. The Pittsfield Fire Department hurried to the scene. Apparently this now-antique fire engine was capable of controlling the fire without assistance. The Capitol Theatre was fortunate to survive the fire with very little damage.

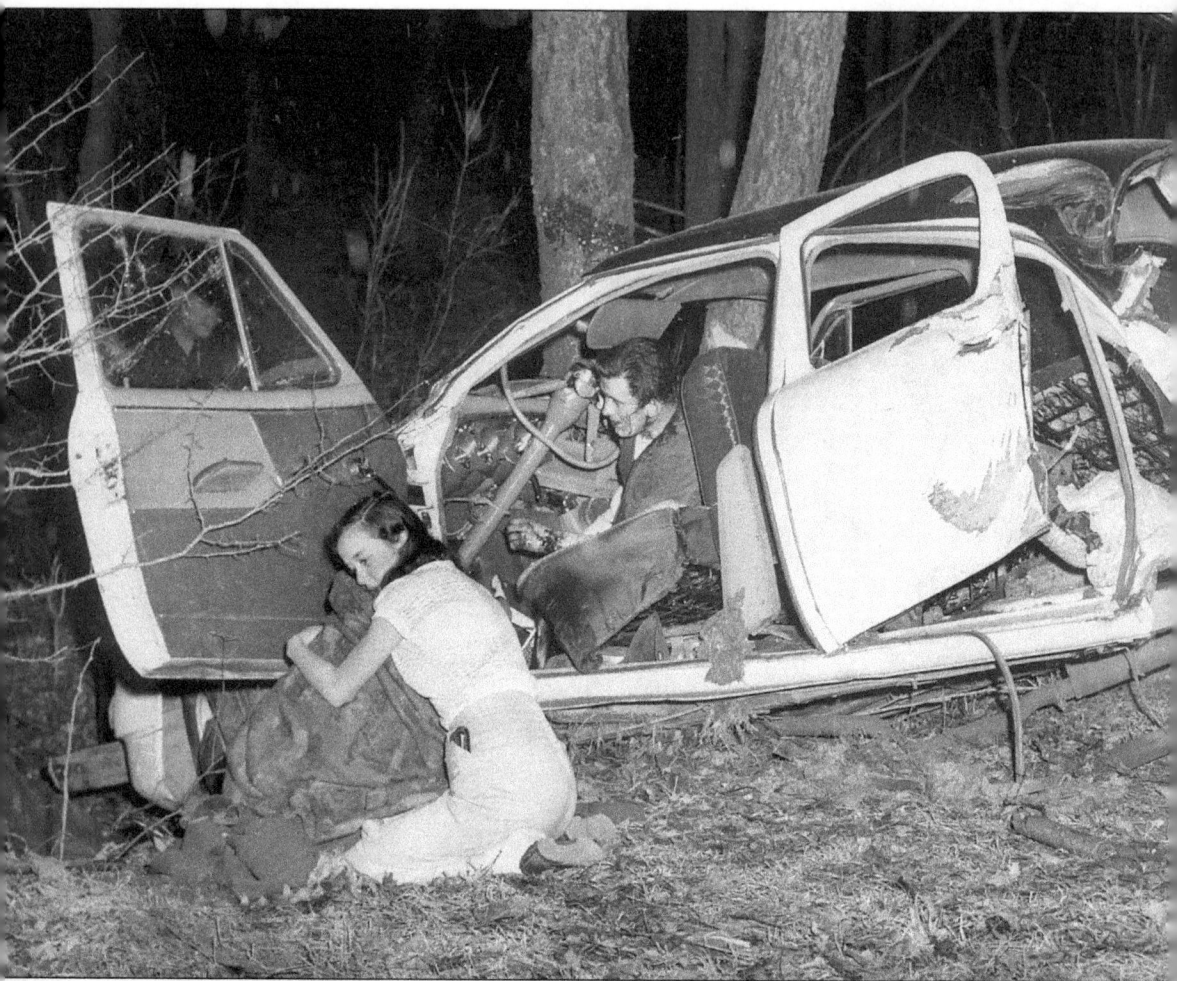

Titled "Roadside Solace," this picture of a car accident on the Mohawk Trail took a first prize in the annual news photo contest of the New England Associated Press News Executive Association. Shown here is Mrs. Bernard Perras holding Agnes LaBombard, who is wrapped in a blanket, just moments after her car went out of control and collided with a utility pole. Right after the accident, Perras had happened along in her own car and stopped to give aid. In the background, still trapped in the car, passenger William Burnash Jr. waits to be rescued. Trabold was on the scene for this picture, apparently ahead of the police and rescue units.

Trabold's 1958 picture of the youthful Sen. John F. Kennedy, shown here with state Sen. Robert P. Cramer and Julius Calvi, later appeared in a 1983 *Transcript* article on the Kennedy presidency. Kennedy scholar and Williams College professor James MacGregor Burns commented, "[Kennedy] won't be remembered for legislative programs as much as he will be remembered as a symbol of hope and excitement."

Photojournalism is the act of portraying a news story with a picture. Two North Adams firefighters, Richard LeFave (with the ax) and James Robare, are inspecting the scene of a fire after the blaze has been put out. Randy has captured these professionals in their element, in the true style of photojournalism.

On the night of January 20, 1977, 21 cars of a 29-car Boston and Maine freight train derailed just east of the old Charlemont railroad station. No one was injured. The derailment blocked South River Road just below the entrance to the Berkshire East ski area. The line was closed for at least two days. Trabold was on the scene to photograph one of the worst accidents experienced by the Boston and Maine Railroad.

Finding the most interesting angle, Randy captures the end of what was once a second home to many teens in North Adams. In the late 1960s, this building's second floor housed the Center, a teen dance club where many gathered. There was often live music or a disc jockey, and it was a fun, safe place to hang out. The first floor of the building was home to the Roberts Company store.

For many years photography was not considered an art form. Randy Trabold knew this was not true. He could look through the lens of his camera and see the perfect form, shadow, pattern, and texture needed to turn an ordinary scene into an extraordinary picture. The Richmond Hotel, located on Main Street in North Adams, closed its doors for the last time in 1958. After most of the furnishings were removed, Randy somehow found his way to this spot to give the community a final glimpse of an urban ruin.

Titled "Helping Hands," this 1957 Trabold photograph received an award in the News Pictures of the Year competition sponsored by the Encyclopedia Britannica. Out of 5,562 entries, Trabold's photograph was one of several selected to join a national traveling exhibition that visited 150 cities. The picture also received a full-page spread in the Toronto *Star Weekly*. The *Star Weekly* caption read, "Fire followed a stove oil explosion in North Adams, Mass., and this unusual photograph shows a housewife who was carried unconscious from her second floor apartment. The blaze swept through four buildings." A later *Transcript* article (April 25, 1958) identified Capt. Esmonde Manson on the ladder receiving the fire victim from firefighter Flyod Sifton (above), who had located the woman in the burning building and carried her to the window.

Six

HOLIDAYS AND CELEBRATIONS

One of the most celebrated aspects of the northern Berkshires is fall foliage, popularized by the annual Fall Foliage Festival parade. Holidays and time with family are important to the people in the communities of northern Berkshire County. These special events bring laughter and create memories. This chapter illustrates the fun side of the region as well as the togetherness that makes the area such a unique place.

Randy Trabold had an eye for capturing moments. He understood how photographs instill memories, whether it was taking part in a first school play or being crowned queen of a festival. As a photojournalist, Trabold reminds us of those magical moments when a community is united in celebration and laughter is a distraction from hardship.

In 1976 people all over the United States celebrated the country's bicentennial. This pint-sized patriot shows her spirit in a Colonial costume as she stands proudly on Center Street in North Adams. Hydrants were painted and all of downtown North Adams shone red, white, and blue as people remembered their forefathers with a parade and a slew of fun events.

Peggy Galipeau parades past the judges in front of the former North Adams National Bank on Main Street. Among 44 other contestants, Galipeau, magnificently clad in a dress resembling autumn leaves, was chosen to be Fall Foliage Queen for the first annual parade that took place on October 8, 1949. As the Drury High School band played, more than 3,000 people gathered near the reviewing stand, desperate to sneak a peek while the judges narrowed down the selection to just 14 women. Representing Richard's Beauty Shop, Galipeau, age 21, was chosen to reign as the year's queen.

Twenty-five years later and without a hair out of place, Peggy Galipeau Grosso stands with her sponsors, Lena and Albert Richards, as they admire the picture of her as Fall Foliage Queen in 1949. Peggy poses here in 1974 in a style that Randy Trabold was fond of: capturing the same pose taken from a picture years earlier. The Richards family owned a beauty salon in North Adams, and Lena Richards did Grosso's hair on both occasions. Just 21 at the time of her inauguration in 1949 and a graduate of Drury High School, she married Edmond Grosso in 1951, owner of the Springs in North Andover. A proud wife and mother, Peggy Grosso, Trabold notes, appears to be the same weight in both photographs.

The Northern Berkshire Chamber of Commerce is a voluntary organization devoted to the business community in the area. Its funding comes from member investments and sponsors. The affiliates create a sense of community by working to improve local businesses through the chamber's six councils: administration, economic development, marketing and communications, membership development, government relations, and education. Over the years the council has served as a sponsor of many Fall Foliage Festival parades and their attendant beauty queens.

Although the Berkshires can often feel like a vast array of mountains stalked by barren winters, something about the beauty of autumn brings an entire community to light during the annual parade in North Adams. Themes have ranged from "Walt Disney," "Freedom," and "Hollywood" to "Music." Children decked out in face paint guzzle root beer, participate in window-painting contests, and gaze wide-eyed at the magnificent floats. The idea was born in 1947, but it was not until 1956 that the parade came to take its present shape. The implementation of fashion shows and election of a festival queen sparked interest.

84

Rowena Humphrey waves to the crowd on Main Street from the top of a float in the 1978 Fall Foliage parade. A former Miss Northern Berkshire, Rowena was crowned Miss Massachusetts, moving on to compete for the Miss America title.

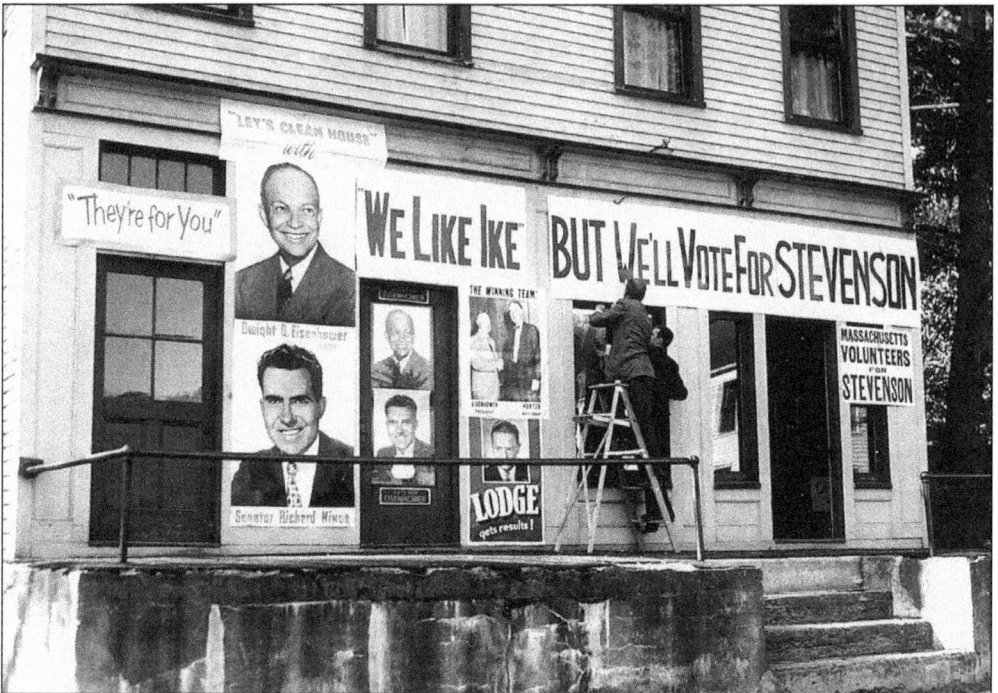

In 1952 Republicans Dwight D. Eisenhower and Richard Nixon ran against Democrats Adlai Stevenson and John Jackson Sparkman. In this storefront in Williamstown, now the Spirit Shop, a few locals politely let their opinions be known. While Stevenson was eventually defeated, the efforts of these two campaign workers did not go unnoticed. This is a great example of Randy Trabold's photojournalistic style. With masterful use of lines and shadows, the photographer captures the excitement of an election as well as a good-natured local feeling.

Every year McCann Technical High School holds a field day on its athletic field. One of the most popular events is the pie-eating contest featured here. Boys of all ages line up for a chance to display their eating abilities.

The results are in, and although locals were pulling for Stevenson, his dream for a "great tomorrow" was crushed.

The Fall Foliage Queen and her court wave to their loyal subjects on Main Street in North Adams in front of the old J.C. Penney store. Joan Davies is shown high on her throne. The others are Angeli Puccio, Helen Hunter, Barbara Milanesi, Sheila Cahoon, Doris Hartman,

and Mrs. Stathes G. Maniatty. Bundled in warm coats, the ladies smile pleasantly, despite the chilling weather.

Peter and Georgette Mancuso wave to the crowd as they ride together in the 1975 Fall Foliage Festival Parade. Peter, a quality control engineer at Sprague Electric, was chairman of the Fall Foliage Festival for twenty years. He was also a volunteer assistant wrestling coach at Drury High School, where Georgette taught home economics. In 1936, Peter was selected for the United States Olympic wrestling team, but injured ribs prevented him from going to Berlin. A one time semi-professional football player as well as a speed skater, he was not only a fine athlete but also a member of the North Adams City Council for two terms.

Dogs of all sizes and breeds squared off for the annual dog show, a part of the Fall Foliage Festival. These two canine rivals size each other up. The dog show added a different element to the usual events at the festival, which included games, food, rides, and of course, the parade.

Onlookers at the Fall Foliage Festival parade watch as this Shriner shows his stuff on the corner of Main and Ashland Streets. In the background is the North Adams Public Library. Each year the North Adams Chamber of Commerce, as well as local schools, Parent-Teacher Associations, and auxiliary clubs, sponsor Fall Foliage events. Clubs and Greek societies from Massachusetts College of Liberal Arts lend a hand also, helping to bridge the gap between college students and townspeople.

These petite Pilgrims have spotted land from their papier-maché *Mayflower*. As part of an annual Thanksgiving celebration, these youngsters have donned their handmade gear and set sail. Randy Trabold loved taking pictures of children, and this is one example of his posed shots. Randy would often set the subjects of his photographs in a way he found striking or comic.

Children and adults lend a hand to touch up the paint on the local Christmas manger scene. At first glance, one cannot tell the figurines from the townspeople sprucing them up. Trabold captures here the friendly atmosphere of the northern Berkshires, one of the things that he admired most about the region.

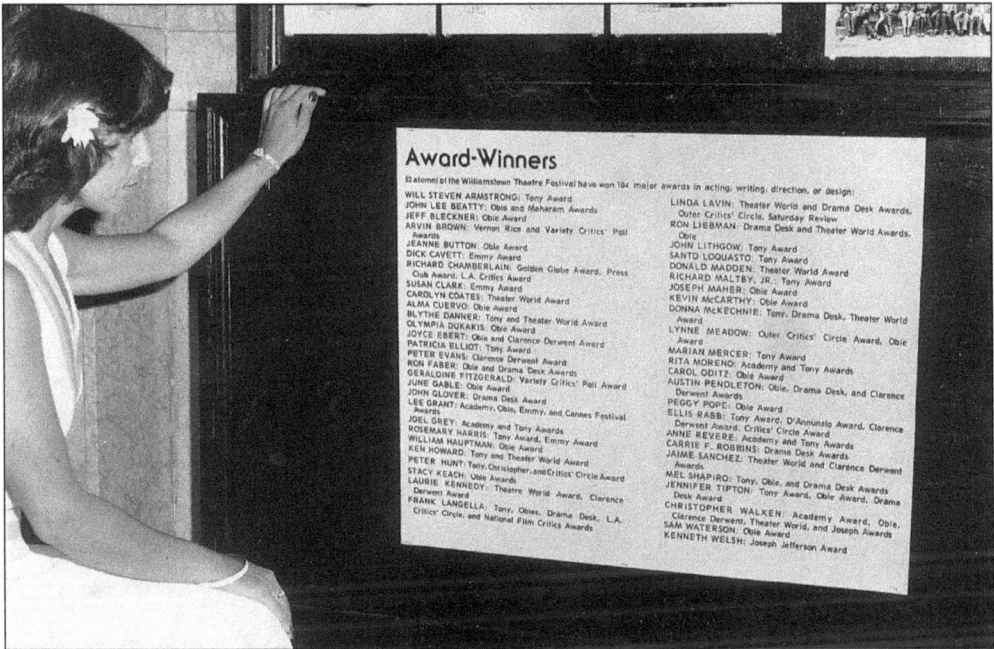

Award-Winners

52 alumni of the Williamstown Theatre Festival have won 104 major awards in acting, writing, direction, or design:

WILL STEVEN ARMSTRONG: Tony Award
JOHN LEE BEATTY: Obie and Maharam Awards
JEFF BLECKNER: Obie Award
ARVIN BROWN: Vernon Rice and Variety Critics' Poll Awards
JEANNE BUTTON: Obie Award
DICK CAVETT: Emmy Award
RICHARD CHAMBERLAIN: Golden Globe Award, Press Club Award, L.A. Critics Award
SUSAN CLARK: Emmy Award
CAROLYN COATES: Theater World Award
ALMA CUERVO: Obie Award
BLYTHE DANNER: Tony and Theater World Award
OLYMPIA DUKAKIS: Obie Award
JOYCE EBERT: Obie and Clarence Derwent Award
PATRICIA ELLIOT: Tony Award
PETER EVANS: Clarence Derwent Award
RON FABER: Obie and Drama Desk Awards
GERALDINE FITZGERALD: Variety Critics' Poll Award
JUNE GABLE: Drama Desk Award
JOHN GLOVER: Drama Desk Award
LEE GRANT: Academy, Obie, Emmy, and Cannes Festival Awards
JOEL GREY: Academy and Tony Awards
ROSEMARY HARRIS: Tony Award, Emmy Award
WILLIAM HAUPTMAN: Obie Award
KEN HOWARD: Tony and Theater World Award
PETER HUNT: Tony, Christopher, and Critics' Circle Award
STACY KEACH: Obie Awards
LAURIE KENNEDY: Theatre World Award, Clarence Derwent Award
FRANK LANGELLA: Tony, Obies, Drama Desk, L.A. Critics' Circle, and National Film Critics Awards

LINDA LAVIN: Theater World and Drama Desk Awards, Outer Critics' Circle, Saturday Review
RON LIEBMAN: Drama Desk and Theater World Awards, Obie
JOHN LITHGOW: Tony Award
SANTO LOQUASTO: Tony Award
DONALD MADDEN: Theater World Award
RICHARD MALTBY, JR.: Tony Award
JOSEPH MAHER: Obie Award
KEVIN McCARTHY: Obie Award
DONNA McKECHNIE: Tony, Drama Desk, Theater World Award
LYNNE MEADOW: Outer Critics' Circle Award, Obie Award
MARIAN MERCER: Tony Award
RITA MORENO: Academy and Tony Awards
CAROL ODITZ: Obie Award
AUSTIN PENDLETON: Obie, Drama Desk, and Clarence Derwent Awards
PEGGY POPE: Obie Award
ELLIS RABB: Tony Award, D'Annunzio Award, Clarence Derwent Award, Critics' Circle Award
ANNE REVERE: Academy and Tony Awards
CARRIE F. ROBBINS: Drama Desk Awards
JAIME SANCHEZ: Theater World and Clarence Derwent Awards
MEL SHAPIRO: Tony, Obie, and Drama Desk Awards
JENNIFER TIPTON: Tony Award, Obie Award, Drama Desk Award
CHRISTOPHER WALKEN: Academy Award, Obie, Clarence Derwent, Theater World, and Joseph Awards
SAM WATERSON: Obie Award
KENNETH WELSH: Joseph Jefferson Award

Referred to as a "theater camp for adults" in a 1988 press conference, the Williamstown Theater Festival has seen many newcomers go on to achieve fame in the theatrical world. Luring stage talent from Christopher Reeve to Sigourney Weaver, the festival opens each spring to provide a special cultural experience for the Berkshire area.

Dr. William H. Everett, president of the Williamstown Theater Festival, proudly stands before the stage on opening night of the summer's productions. The 2002 Tony Award Festival has seen more than 500 productions, workshops, and special events since it opened its doors in 1955. The 520-seat Adams Memorial Theater serves as the main stage. For 11 weeks from June to August, the Berkshires become a bustling array of theatrical talent and star-struck fans.

The Skydiver is always a fun part of the Fall Foliage Festival's carnival. Set in the urban renewal lot (now Brooks), this giant Ferris wheel climbs high into the sky on a sparkling fall day. Trabold captures the dark and light in the sky and clouds, as well as the juxtaposition of the angular base of the wheel against its round top, to create a compelling artistic photograph.

94

Seven

WINTER

It all starts in the fall, as thousands of people visit the northern Berkshires to view the leaves changing colors. By the first snowfall, open fields are marked with cross-country skiing tracks, golf courses turn into hills for sledding, and the lakes become perfect places for skating and ice fishing. For those still searching for breathtaking scenery, sunshine makes settled snowflakes twinkle and glisten like Christmas lights. The whole area becomes a winter wonderland.

As a resident of northern Berkshire County, Randy Trabold knew how important winter was for the region. He knew that snow changed the appearance of the area dramatically. The contrast of textures between the bark of a tree and the shimmering surface of fresh snow was not only aesthetically pleasing but also artistically interesting. Transportation adapted to the elements; cars either slowed down or suffered the consequences, and sleighs conquered the unplowed rough roads. Winter was also a time for Randy to warm the chill with some of his characteristic humor.

Unforgiving winter winds give this tree a skin of snow, as harsh light illuminates the new flesh. In this composition, Randy uses the striking sunlight to create a series of contours, much like an Ansel Adams photograph. Adams often used light and dark to create a smooth contour line. The contour in this image is not completely smooth, but the texture of the snow creates a bright outline to contrast the horizontal fluff of cloud behind the tree. This winter abstraction is actually a closeup of a branch hanging from a sign-posted tree on the Bellows Pipe Trail in Mount Greylock State Park.

This picture, dated March 23, 1977, shows an example of the kind of massive snowfall Berkshire residents have to face in the winter. Here, Sean Bishop of Florida, Massachusetts, son of Walter Bishop, shovels off the top of his father's car after a late snowstorm added more than 12 inches of new snow to what had already fallen. Stuck near the road, the Bishop family car would not find itself back at the top of the Bishops' long driveway for a long time.

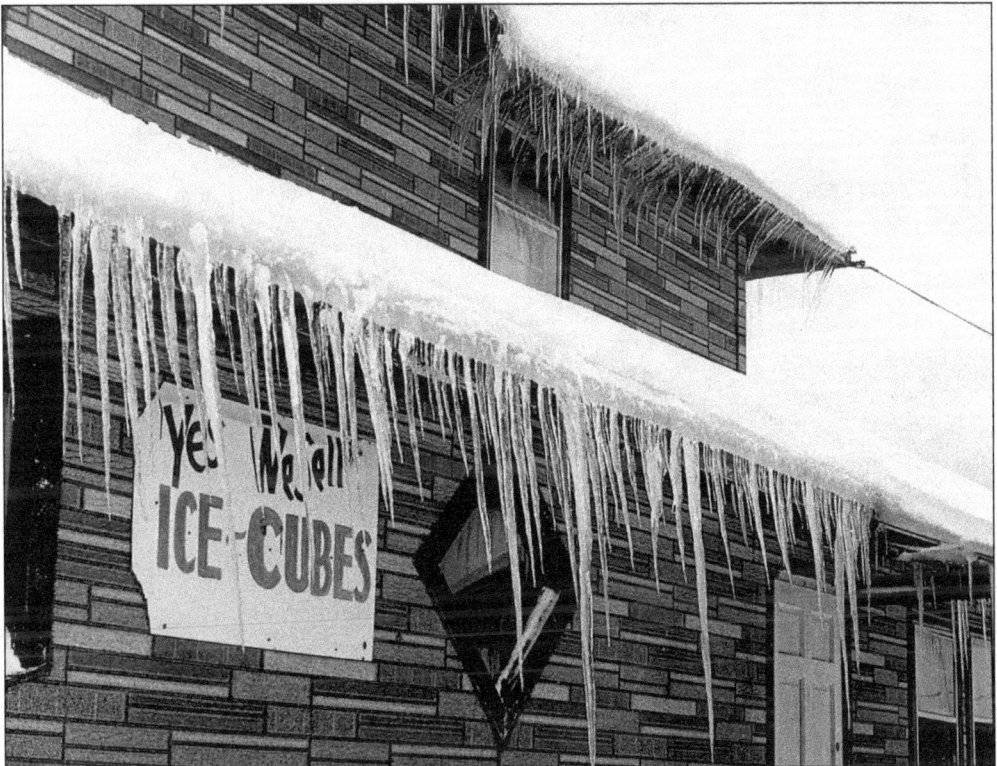

In this photograph of Matt's Lodge in Savoy, Massachusetts, Randy shows us his sense of comic irony. Not only is this building covered in snow and draped in frozen stalactites, but ice cubes are sold here, too.

Here Randy Trabold beautifully captures Butch Wildman in the middle of a ski jump. The sharp diagonal of the ski captures the dynamism and athletic difficulty of the jump. Butch was truly a "Wildman." He is only using one ski here because he has fractured his other foot, but despite the injury, he appears capable of doing his usual stunts with no fear about damaging his already broken foot.

The churches of North Adams give the city a distinctive skyline. Randy Trabold builds a composition that forces a comparison between the architectural beauty of the steeples and the mountainlike shape of a snow mound.

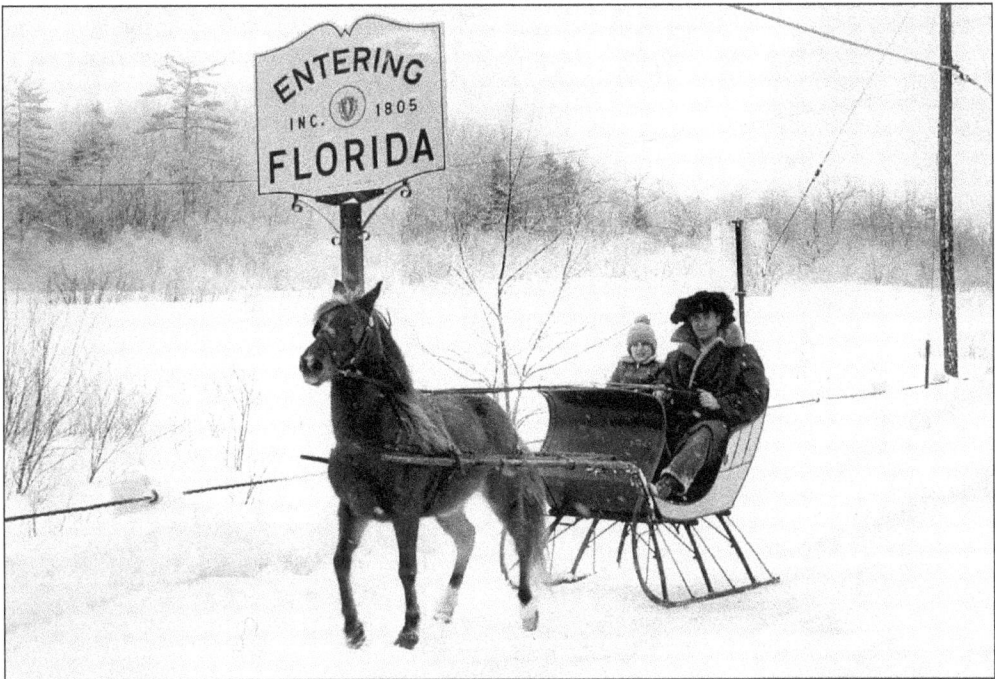

Titled "Sleigh Bells in Florida," this is one of many signature Trabold pictures using the "Entering Florida" sign at the top of the Mohawk Trail as a prop for visual irony. Adolph J. Heideman and his 10-year-old son, James, make their way through a snow-covered Florida, Massachusetts, with their pony Bambi leading the way.

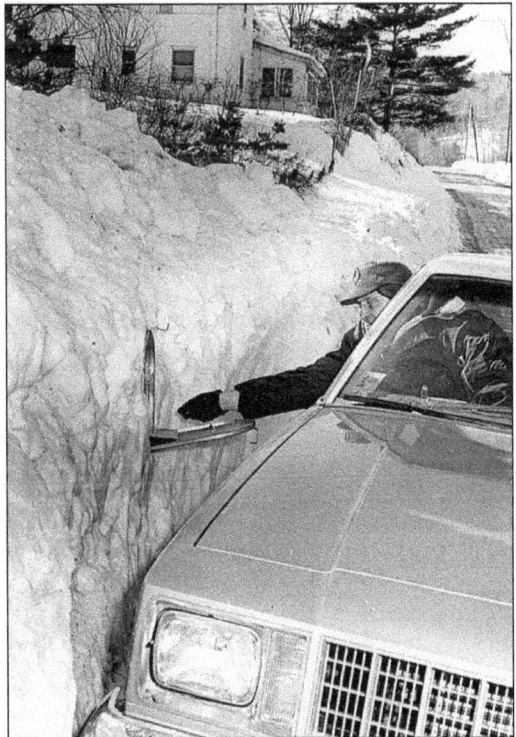

Here a gentleman on Eagle Street has to make quite a stretch from his car to get his mail. At least, his mailbox is encased in a mountain of snow that may keep it safe from wandering plows.

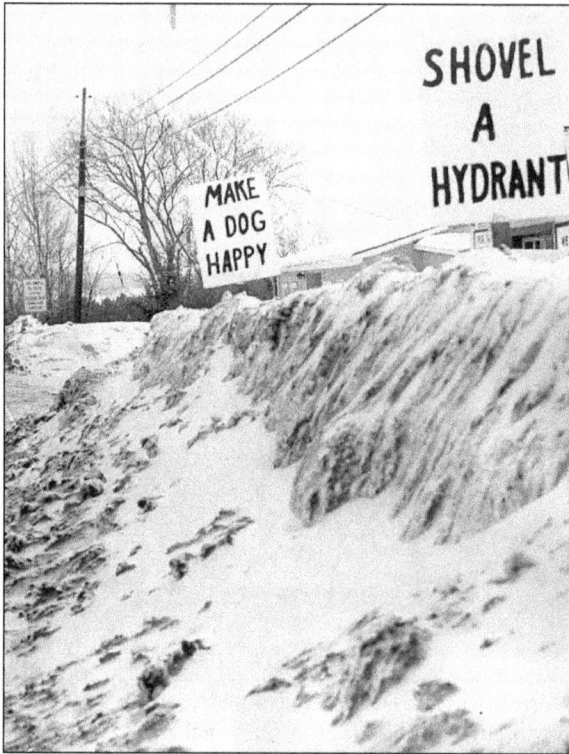

The big snowplows in the Berkshire area have a scoop design that tosses snow high to the side. The faster the driver goes, the farther and higher the snow is thrown. In their snow-removal race pictured here, the snowplows have inadvertently buried a fire hydrant, and it looks like the neighborhood dogs may just have to be patient until summer.

A seasonal event for the area is the formation of massive icicles on the exposed rockface of the Hairpin Turn on Route 2 in Clarksburg. The combination of melting snow, rain, and groundwater spill out of the rockface and freeze into icicles and onto the road, sometimes making the highway into an ice rink that spans the dangerous turn. This photograph shows an unidentified man picking a ripe icicle. He is silhouetted against the glittering wall and stands at the bottom of the picture. Trabold's composition demonstrates the impressive size of the rockface and the ice that blooms on it.

This winter monstrosity is actually a sprinkler or a fountain left on during the winter so that it would not freeze and be damaged. The constant spraying water created layer upon layer of ice, eventually growing to large proportions.

The Beware of Dog sign shown here contrasts with the dog itself, who looks cute and insignificant against a massive bank of snow. He also seems doomed to become the victim of a falling icicle.

101

Frozen to the ground on the sidewalk of River Street, just west of Houghton Street in North Adams, this cart looks as though it has been victimized by the frozen food section of a supermarket.

Rain gutters are used to channel water off the roof and keep icicles from forming. Occasionally, especially in areas populated with many trees, leaves fall into the gutters and plug them up. If a clog is allowed to stay in the gutter through the winter, stagnant water can turn into miniature ice floes. In this view of Phelps Dodge, people cannot even get to the door to apply for the advertised jobs.

In a photograph titled "Miami Bound," Randy's daughter Barbara Cirone poses for him beneath the sign he made famous. Trabold's "Entering Florida" series began in 1939 and ran for 40 years until he retired in 1979. During that time Randy experimented with a number of variations on the theme. As he wrote to his friend J. Walter Green, Associated Press wire service photo editor, "One year I used a Santa, another year . . . a sleigh, another year . . . a sleigh with a Santa; I have used girls in bathing suits under the sign; one year the snow was so deep there I had a man straddling the sign with snowshoes."

In the late 1960s, Randy Trabold captured the beauty of a dealer's lot with new Ford cars enshrouded in snow. When viewed as a whole, the mass of cars, aided by the snowfall, is transformed into an undulating form that narrows as the cars near the horizon. The line in the background where the cars end and the trees and mountains begin divides the photograph into two nearly equal parts. Here, Trabold turned a picture of a car dealership into a work of art.

In nearly symmetrical composition, these icicles hide a second-story porch as winter sunlight permeates the frozen giants and creates a shimmering cascade of light onto the deck below. This photograph demonstrates the power of the camera to capture the seemingly endless variety of the natural world.

Eight

MASSACHUSETTS COLLEGE
OF LIBERAL ARTS

Massachusetts College of Liberal Arts (MCLA) is a small liberal arts college with approximately 1,500 undergraduate and graduate students. Settled in the northern Berkshires, it is one of nine state colleges within the state's educational system. Enclosed by gorgeous mountains and hills, the college is located in the city of North Adams. In 1894 it was established and known as North Adams Normal School. Thirty-eight years later, the school became the State Teachers College at North Adams and was certified to have a four-year curriculum that granted bachelor of science degrees in education. The college was designated North Adams State College in 1960 to recognize its diversification, which included majors in business administration as well as the liberal arts. It was officially named Massachusetts College of Liberal Arts in 1997, in recognition of the school's new mission to become a premier state liberal arts college. Throughout the school's history, MCLA has given students a liberal arts education as well as skills in professional leadership.

MCLA was an interesting topic for Randy Trabold, because the school provided opportunities for superb feature photographs and because his wife, Ida, is a distinguished alumna. Through Randy Trabold's camera, the community had an opportunity to share what was happening at MCLA, whether it was moving-in day, graduation, sports activities, or a variety of interesting and enjoyable events. In the spring of 1979, Randy was honored by MCLA with the establishment of a journalism scholarship in his name. The citation from acting president Anthony Ceddia read in part, "[This scholarship] is established in grateful recognition for your long-term coverage of the institution, and out of respect for the state-of-the-art you represent."

The quadrangle at Massachusetts College of Liberal Arts is pictured c. 1975. It is an area where students and teachers can enjoy events such as convocation and graduation as well as leisurely lunches and open-air classes. The quad is enclosed by Bowman Hall, Eldridge Hall, Freel Library, and the Venable Gym. At the left rear is the Amsler Campus Center. It houses the college cafeteria, new gymnasium, student affairs offices, and the fitness area. Bowman Hall stands at the right rear. It houses chemistry, math, and physics departments, as well as the fine and performing arts studios, various offices, and classrooms. In 1998 the quad was renovated. Old walkways and benches were removed, brick and concrete paths laid, and bushes and trees planted to improve the appearance of the campus.

Crowds of students lounge in a field at Windsor Lake (nicknamed the Fish Pond). The event, called Spring Fling, was a favorite, giving students a chance to escape campus and relax. Much later, Spring Fling became an on-campus event centering around activities and music. The picture below shows the aftermath of Spring Fling, a condition still prevalent at today's event: lots of trash.

Cement, waffle-like blocks are laid down between rows of townhouses to make a walkway. This area, still called "the fire lane," connects Montana Street to Ashland Street through the townhouse complex. It was built to allow fire truck access to the townhouse complex. More than just a walkway, this area has seen barbecues and even the occasional pickup game of baseball. The large building in the background is Murdock Hall, the oldest building on campus, dating back to 1894.

College protesters carry Michael Gorman (in wheelchair) up the stairs in front of Venable Hall. This October 24, 1975 event was covered by Trabold for the *North Adams Transcript*. Today this and just about every other area of the campus has wheelchair-accessible ramps.

Students interact in front of the Massachusetts College of Liberal Arts's Flagg Townhouses c. 1978. Completed in 1976, the townhouses were named in honor of Andrew Sinclair Flagg. Flagg was an art faculty member at the college from 1937 to 1966. He became the college's sixth president in 1966 and remained in that position for three years.

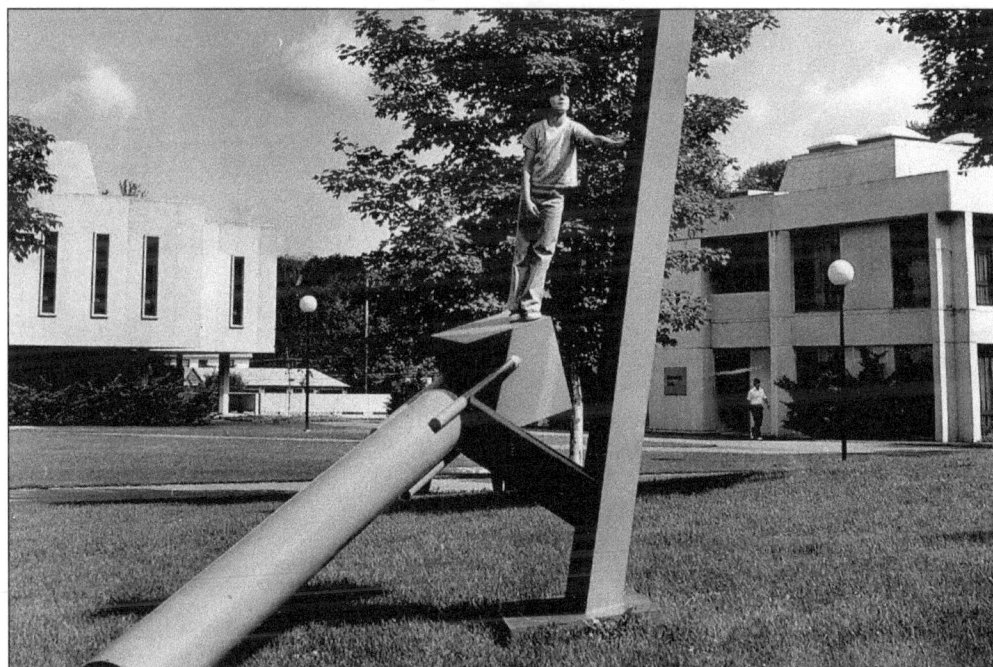

Here is a photograph of *Genesis*, a sculpture by Ailine Shulman of Averill Park, New York. This sculpture was acquired in the late fall of 1976 by George Jarck of the art department. *Genesis* is a constructionist abstract steel sculpture. The work was on display until 1978 in the campus quad in front of Bowman Hall.

A student uses his free time on a sunny day to perfect his skateboarding tricks. The building behind him is Mark Hopkins School, an elementary school on the campus grounds. It is now called Mark Hopkins Hall and houses the education department, computer labs, as well as a television studio.

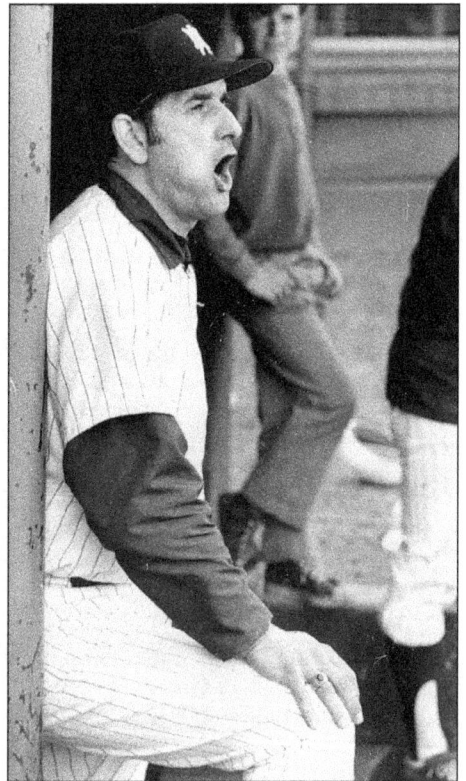

Baseball made its way to Massachusetts College of Liberal Arts as an official sport in 1950. Here is baseball coach Joe Zavattaro, who became the school's coach in 1963 and retired in 1995. This photograph marks the team's first home baseball game during the spring season of 1970. The team played against Johnson State and won 3-0. During Zavattaro's 32 years as coach, the baseball team played 811 games, winning 497 of them. With his guidance, MCLA made it to numerous postseason tournaments, winning the MASCAC championship 11 times.

Here James T. Amsler, the seventh president of Massachusetts College of Liberal Arts, salutes a graduating student c. 1975. As president, Amsler helped many undergraduates by giving them an unprecedented voting voice on every college governing committee; he also encouraged hundreds of students to branch out into the community to work on social betterment projects or political campaigns. Amsler was one of the presidents who helped change the school from a teacher-oriented institution into one that is professional as well as liberal arts in orientation. In 1994 the Massachusetts College of Liberal Arts campus center was named in his honor.

Shown here is the taping of the program *Super Consumer* at the first television studio of Massachusetts College of Liberal Arts. The show focused on consumer issues and aired on Channel 7, a northern Berkshires station. The television studio debuted in 1976 and was located in the English and communications department on the second floor of Murdock Hall. In 2003 the studio was relocated in the basement of Mark Hopkins. At the pitch board is Steve Smallman, the program director of *Super Consumer.* On the right is Mary Daily, the "super consumer," and operating the camera is Bonnie Leonard.

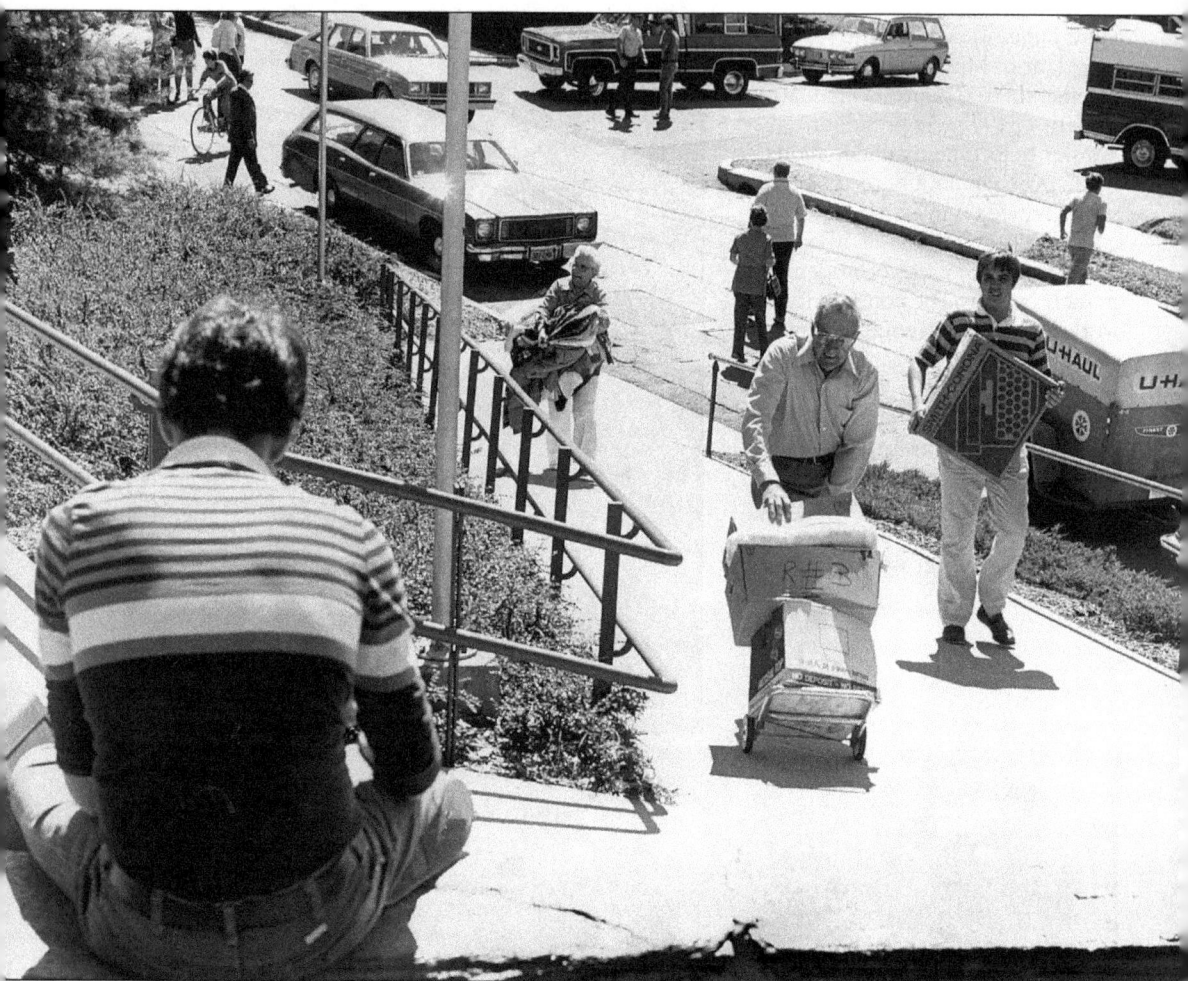

Freshman students move into the Berkshire Towers in the mid-1970s. While nowadays students lug computers and printers up the cement walkway, the student in the picture carries an electric typewriter. The Berkshire Towers have eight floors of student housing, with 13 single or double rooms on each floor.

In 1978 Massachusetts College of Liberal Arts lost one of the oldest and most beautiful buildings on campus, Taconic Hall. Taconic Hall was built in 1903, just nine years after the college opened. Along with Smith House and Murdock Hall, it was one of the original buildings. Taconic Hall was known as a men's dormitory and also included a theater and the college cafeteria, both located in the basement. To some it was home for four years; to others it was a historical landmark. A lawn bearing its name and a parking lot take the place of Taconic Hall today.

Finding a place to park is never easy at Massachusetts College of Liberal Arts, especially if you are a student. This photograph, taken c. 1976, displays one of the student parking lots located on the east side of Taconic Hall before the building was demolished in 1978. Hoosac Hall, an all-girls dormitory opened in 1966, faces the parking lot. The parking lot, paved and landscaped with trees and bushes, still exists today.

Here is a photograph taken from Freel Library parking lot at Massachusetts College of Liberal Arts *c.* 1973. Randy Trabold's approach to photojournalism here is narrated through a precise and accurate form. The architecture of the buildings is square, contrasting with the oval shapes of the cars. The low-angle position of the camera leads the focus upward toward the photograph's vanishing point and focuses attention on the skyline. What makes this photograph remarkable are the shadows and lighting that give it a dramatic, three-dimensional look.

Nine

PEOPLE IN ACTION

Each corner of northern Berkshire County has a twist, turn, and surprise awaiting discovery, just as the personalities of the people in these photographs do. From little children being themselves to adults being like little children, these photographs are packed with fun. Some of the pictures take on a more serious note, demonstrating life at its utmost, both the good times and the bad. This chapter is a brief sampling of the life of people in the Berkshires.

Whether his photographs were candid or posed, Randy Trabold had an eye for comedy as well as human concern. His love of children being silly made for some perfect little-kid shots. He also happened upon many adults being amusing: their daring deeds while working and clever advertisements for help. Randy Trabold caught it all with his camera.

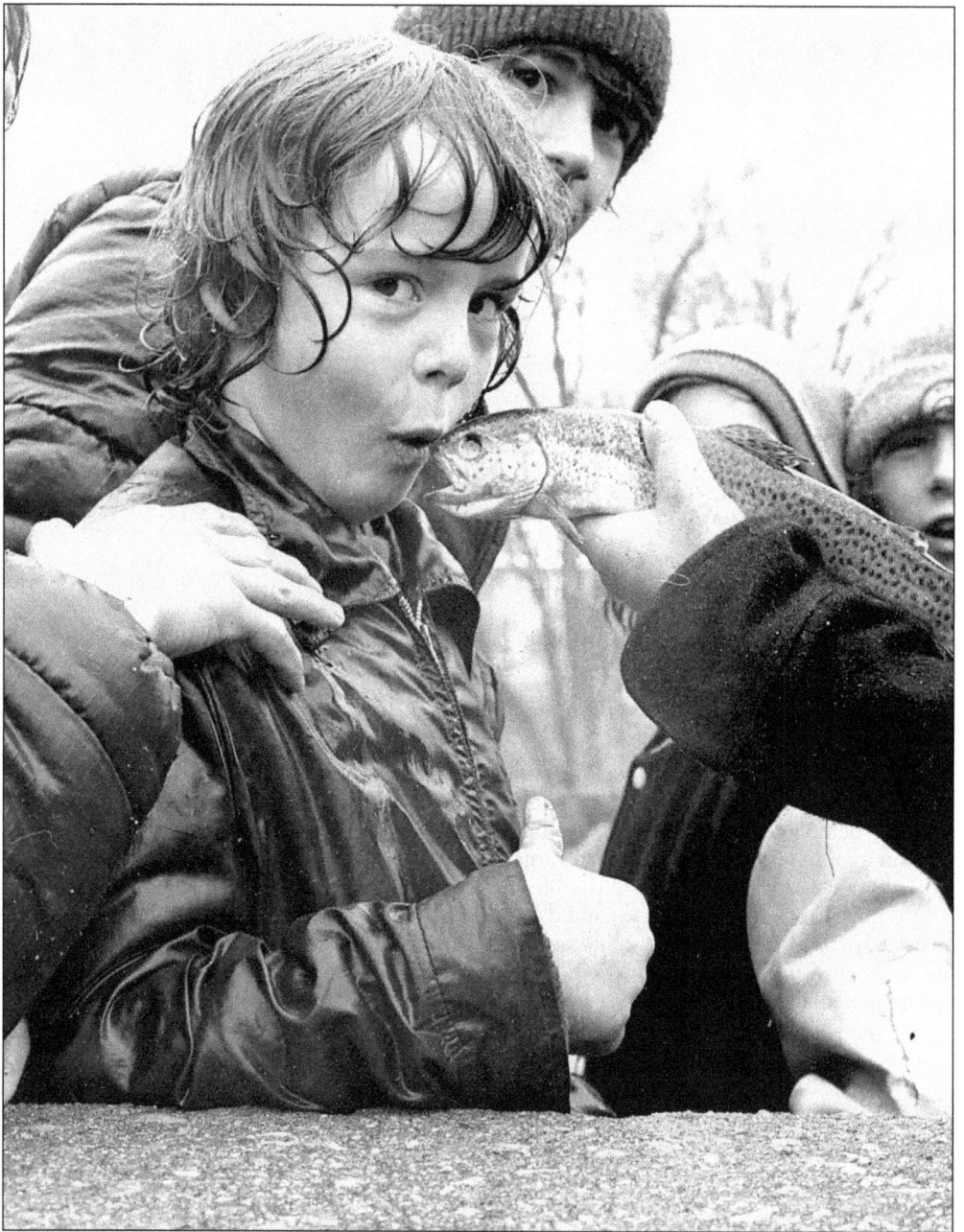

Randy Trabold seemed to have an innate ability to capture the spirit of youth. Here some young men are having fun on a fishing trip. Trabold captures a human-interest moment as one of the boys poses to kiss his catch.

After three and a half years of service, Wiggins Airway, "the Community Airline," is preparing for its last flight. Pilot Harry F. Otterm (left) of Albany, New York, and Mohawk Aviation mechanic John Hyde are seen here giving the plane a final inspection. Otterm flew this plane each day for those three and a half years. The flights included two daily trips between Albany and Boston. The airway was forced to close because of falling passenger use.

On February 4, 1948, the Harriman Airport in North Adams opened. The airport was named after Lottie Mae Harriman (seen here cutting the ribbon), the first female member of the North Adams City Council. Also shown in the photograph are, from left to right, the president of the North Adams City Council, Robert Temple; Dr. Cyril P. Rosston; and Reed Barrons.

It is 1938, and George Herman "Babe" Ruth is playing in a twilight game at Noel Field. Located in North Adams, Noel Field hosted a variety of sports events from the beginning of the 20th century. This game pitted the Brooklyn Dodgers against an all-star Sons of Italy, Lodge No. 704 team. Then a coach for the Dodgers and near the end of his major-league career, Ruth played first base. The Babe is captured here by Trabold's camera as he prepares to bat at home plate before an estimated crowd of 3,500.

Many years later, at the same Noel Field, these three boys are apparently the only ones who still want to play ball after a snowstorm. Their enthusiasm that day might well have been fueled in part by the lingering spirit of "the Great Bambino."

The North Adams Fire Department gives a demonstration to some local elementary school children on safety precautions when jumping from a burning building. The photograph is a quintessential Trabold action shot. He perfectly captures the fun in this event, which is what the firemen were trying to achieve within the framework of a serious subject. Joe Delisle is captured midair while showing the children how easily it is done.

Three members of the Bedard Brothers Racing Team are shown with one of their Saabs, "the Well Built Swede." Leo Bedard (left), Ron Bedard (center), and John Kondel show off their racing trophies to Randy Trabold in this picture, taken in the late 1960s. The brothers earned their trophies from racing Saab automobiles on the frozen Cheshire Lake during the New England ice-racing season. The cars were equipped with non-studded snow tires. New England ice-racing began in New Hampshire and Maine, but the Bedard brothers brought it to the northern Berkshires.

William E. Hoellerich of Adams poses with an airplane that he constructed himself. Randy Trabold referred to Hoellerich's creation as "the homemade plane." During the photographic session, Hoellerich flew the airplane so that Randy could also take some action shots. At the time, no one at the *Transcript* had approached Hoellerich to do a story about his airplane. Trabold would often initiate news stories such as this with his photography.

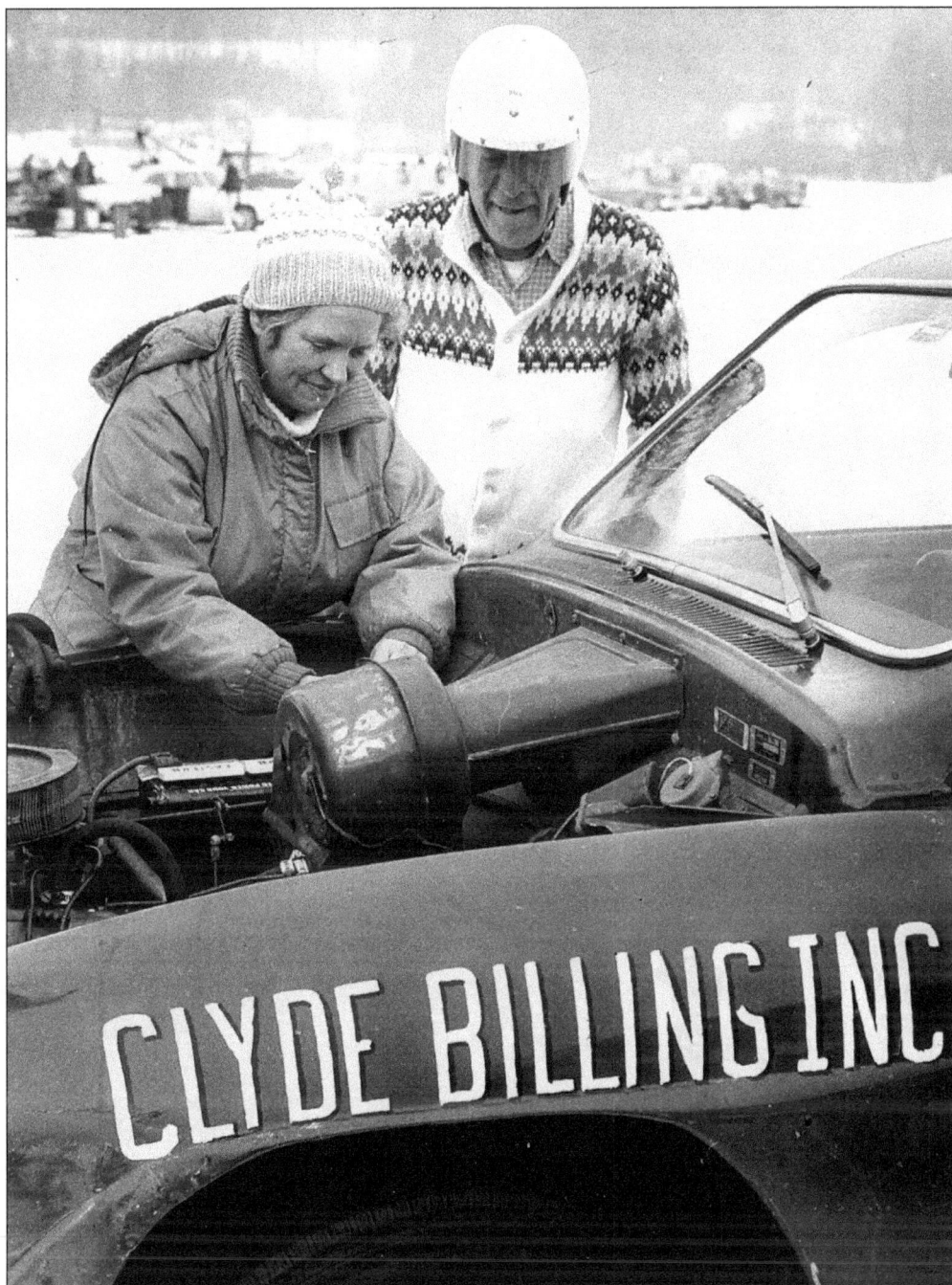

Clyde Billings of Framingham, Maine, watches as his wife and "pit boss" checks his car before the start of a race. Billings was the New England ice-racing champion for many years and has been named "the Grand Old Man of Ice-Racing."

The use of light and shadow in this picture is what makes it so compelling. The brightness and vastness of the clouds make the sky appear to go on forever. The contrast of the clouds and shadowed figure of the golfer allows us to see his artful form.

In this photograph, Randy Trabold has found a daredevil disguised as a city worker. The location is just below the overpass on Marshall Street near the former Sprague Electric factories. Trabold certainly had an eye for interesting predicaments.

Fred Schwarzer seems busy in this photograph of the Williamstown telephone switchboard from the 1930s. With this photograph, Randy brings us back to a time when people had to be manually connected by the operator to the person they were calling.

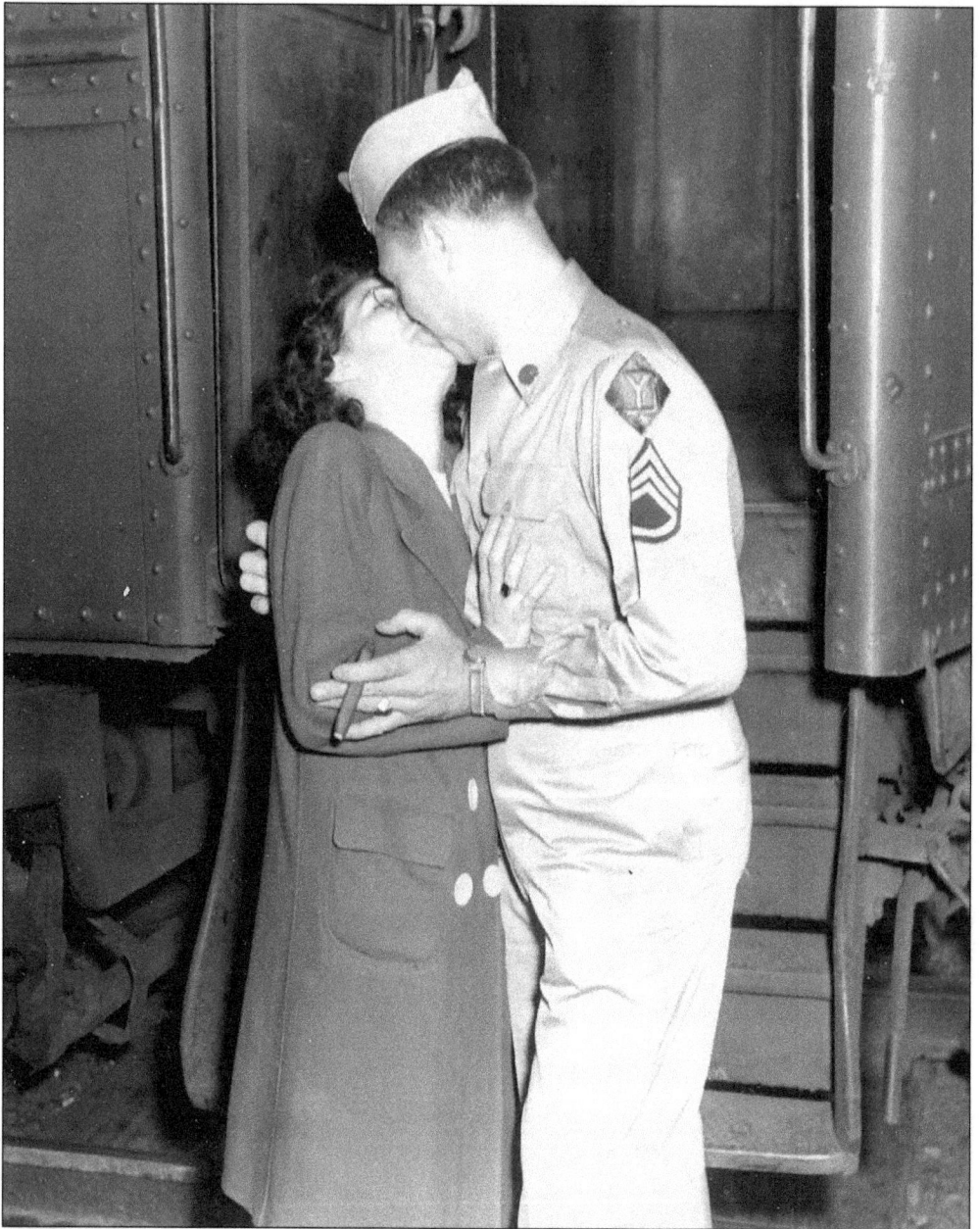

Trabold captures an unidentified couple in a timeless pose, reminiscent of the famous V-J Day photograph by Alfred Eisenstaedt of a sailor and nurse embracing in Times Square.

The joys of painting are not always as abundant as they are necessary. Randy Trabold captured the human interest as well as the humor in this photograph of John and Jim Bishop painting the family house, located on West Main Street in North Adams. John Bishop remembers painting the house for weeks, and one night as he was finishing, he decided to paint a request. The very next morning, Randy Trabold knocked on the door and asked if he could take a picture. The boys fell into a heap of trouble with their mother, who did not know about the public request.

Three generations of the Gould family prepare to run in the annual North Adams Marathon. The race started at State Street, where the women are getting ready. Randy never missed an opportunity to capture little ones at their best. Here he catches the family's five-year-old proudly wearing her mother's number for her first marathon.

Living life a little dangerously, Randy has found a young man in the midst of a popular Berkshire pastime, kayaking. This award-winning sports picture was taken by Trabold on May 20, 1959. Shooting the rapids of the Green River is John B. Reid Jr. of Williams College.

One of Trabold's more somber photographs is seen here. He has captured a grave and emotional moment. Pfc. Peter A. Cook's picture is on the mantel, between his widow and the high-ranking officer who is presenting her with Cook's medals of honor. On the left is the Air Medal, given for meritorious achievement while participating in aerial flight. On the right is the Purple Heart, given for wounds received in action.

Here Trabold has wonderfully captured the solemnity of two young boys praying at the altar of one of the many Catholic churches in North Adams. The ascension of dark to light gives the feeling of a Italian Renaissance painting. Trabold's understanding of both photography and art is well displayed in this composition.

After 43 years beginning in 1936, Randy Trabold pauses before covering his final Williams College commencement. Shown here with commencement speaker Terris Moore (left) and Williams College president John Chandler, Randy was honored with a retrospective exhibition of his Williams College commencement photographs at the Williams College Museum of Art. Chandler observed, "Through his photography of northern Berkshire scenes and events, Randy Trabold has become the author of a significant part of our region's history."

Visit us at
arcadiapublishing.com